CLASSICAL GUITAR CHOPS

Essential Licks & Exercises to Maximize Your Technique

BY EVAN HIRSCHELMAN

I would like to dedicate this book to my parents.

To access audio visit:
www.halleonard.com/mylibrary

Enter Code
5564-2125-1877-4424

ISBN 978-1-4584-0423-7

HAL•LEONARD®

7777 W. BLUEMOUND RD. P.O. BOX 13819 MILWAUKEE, WI 53213

In Australia Contact:
Hal Leonard Australia Pty. Ltd.
4 Lentara Court
Cheltenham, Victoria, 3192 Australia
Email: ausadmin@halleonard.com.au

Visit Hal Leonard Online at
www.halleonard.com

1 Part I: Licks and Musical Passages

60 Part II: Historical Exercises

Foreword

To keep me well away from the other competent players, the high school orchestra director saw fit to seat me in the last chair of the 2nd violin section. Although I thought I wasn't too bad of a violinist for a guitar player, it seems the majority of those around me thought I should stick to guitar and discontinue the violin—immediately! Odd, but I was always convinced that it was the bow that made all the racket! The violin was just fine.

Since my high school years, a great many of my friends throughout life have been orchestral musicians. I've been around them when they were working hard on their excerpts for this or that audition. As a soloist, I used to think it was strange that I never heard them actually play through an entire piece of music—that they could actually secure employment from knowing, primarily, excerpts from famous orchestral standards.

It later dawned on me that we do tend to compare and rate a musician based on how one plays a well-known passage. As a guitarist and teacher, I realized in my own practice that one can greatly improve one's technical abilities and musical understanding by focusing on excerpts from pieces. I've always been a big believer in the "divide and conquer" path to mastering something, and in music, that boils down to dividing a piece of music into sections and extracting its most challenging areas.

In *Classical Guitar Chops*, that is exactly what the author, and my friend and colleague, Evan Hirschelman, has done. In its pages, you will be encouraged to gain mastery over some of the guitar's best-loved repertoire by focusing on the excerpts that demand the most attention. With his detailed guidance, you will find yourself overcoming obstacles easily and quickly, practicing the sections that need the work. And, besides, it's fun going to the creamy center right away!

Classical Guitar Chops is the book I wish I had when I was starting to evolve as a player. It is a book that is long overdue, authored by a master teacher and extraordinary guitarist and musician. Practice what he says and enjoy the rewards.

I wish you much joyous music-making,

Scott Tennant
Pasadena, CA

About the Author

An award-winning guitarist and composer, Evan Hirschelman has gained international acclaim for his unique compositions, virtuosic performances, and dynamic interpretational renditions. He has been heralded for "precise and prodigious technique" by *Acoustic Guitar* magazine, "technical wizardry" by the *Los Angeles Times*, and "soulful musicality" by the *Malibu Times*. Whether performing original compositions, traditional classical repertoire, or exploring diverse musical forms, Hirschelman seeks to find connections that stimulate the imagination.

As a composer, Hirschelman's compositions reflect a fusion of musical influences. They range from classical to metal, creating a unique style of hybrid music hailed by critics and audiences alike. He has been commissioned by renowned musicians and received top accolades for his composing. The Grammy award-winning recording *Guitar Heroes* includes Hirschelman's composition "Lament and Wake," performed by the preeminent Los Angeles Guitar Quartet. His compositions are included in the new edition of the seminal classical guitar book *Pumping Nylon* and his solo and ensemble works have been performed by musicians throughout the world.

His recording *Water in Darkness* contains original and contemporary solo guitar works and duets with guitarist Scott Tennant. It was released to rave reviews, being called "complex and breathtaking" by *Music Connection*, "delightful and virtuosic" by *American Record Guide*, and a "two-handed symphony" by *Minor 7th*. Hirschelman has been featured in guitar's foremost publications, including *Classical Guitar*, *Acoustic Guitar*, and *Guitar Player*. He has been a top prize winner in multiple guitar competitions, including the renowned Stotsenberg International Guitar Competition.

As an educator, Hirschelman is frequently in demand for masterclasses and workshops. He has served on the faculty at several colleges, including the Musicians Institute, and currently runs a thriving private teaching studio. Hirschelman is the author of *Acoustic Artistry: Tapping, Slapping, and Percussion Techniques for Classical & Fingerstyle Guitar*, published by Hal Leonard Corporation. Its international popularity has quickly grown, and as a result it has been translated to multiple languages by De Haske Publications, Europe.

A native of Detroit, Michigan, Evan Hirschelman currently resides in Los Angeles, where he divides his time between composing, performing, and teaching music. He holds a Master of Music degree from the University of Southern California and a Bachelor of Music degree from the University of Arizona.

Evan Hirschelman resides on the web at **www.theguitarist.net**.

Credits

Recorded and Mixed at Olive Tree Studio, Pasadena, CA
Guitar by Kenny Hill, Signature (lattice/double top)
Photos by Dario Griffin

Acknowledgments

I would like to thank: Jeff Schroedl, Kurt Plahna, and everyone at Hal Leonard for their support; Ken Nagatani for his advice and editing; Kevin Langan, Patrick McClanahan, and Willem Cilliers for their helpful comments; Scott Tennant for his input while developing this book idea.

...and most importantly, my parents, who were instrumental in developing my musical tendencies.

Preface

Classical Guitar Chops was designed to help develop technique through the study of classical guitar excerpts and historical exercises. A wide array of conventional techniques within the classical guitar repertoire are covered, including slurs, arpeggios, tremolo, scalar lines, natural and artificial harmonics, contrapuntal lines, shifting, campanella, barring, string dampening, and many more.

Works by Bach, Guiliani, Paganini, Albéniz, and other important composers from the 17th century onwards are included. The musical examples draw from notable passages in each composition. Each excerpt is preceded by an analysis of the respective techniques required and suggestions are offered to solve the most common issues. By isolating portions of each piece, the reader is able to focus on specific technical requirements as separate entities, allowing a more focused context for practicing. In addition to developing technique, you will gain a more thorough knowledge of classical guitar literature, along with the added musicianship that comes with it.

Guitarists of varying skill levels can benefit from this book, since it covers a large cross-section of repertoire and techniques, but the book will be most beneficial to students of intermediate level and above. The chosen examples contain varying technical and musical challenges, but a common thread throughout the repertoire in this publication is a tendency towards virtuosic passages. This book is not meant to be studied in chronological order; rather, the reader is encouraged to skip around according to their specific interests.

Important exercises by Carcassi, Giuliani, and Tárrega are also included. These exercises are indispensable in developing finger independence, speed, and agility, among other benefits. By integrating these studies into your daily practice routine, you will encounter a large group of technical permutations that will help develop both hands. Before each group of exercises, I offer suggestions to aid the implementation of the required techniques into your practice sessions. For certain studies, I also offer fingering and harmonic variations to ease the repetitious nature of extended periods of practicing.

Each musical passage is recorded on the accompanying audio. The examples are meant for demonstration purposes and not to be mimicked exactly. The interpretation of classical repertoire should vary between performers. One of the most interesting facets of performing music written by other composers is adding your own "touch" within the context of their musical style and voice.

In addition to practicing out of this book, you are highly encouraged to study with a competent instructor. This interaction will help you address specific technical issues and develop an interpretational vocabulary in classical music, which in turn will lead to musical maturity. It is my hope that this book, in conjunction with private study, will help your guitar playing become more fluent and inventive.

All the best,
Evan Hirschelman

A Note on Music Notation

This book contains tablature in addition to standard music notation. The publisher and the author felt it would be beneficial to include tablature for intermediate level students, whose fluency in note reading across the fingerboard positions might not be advanced enough to tackle many of the excerpts included in this book.

The top line of music (standard notation) will include left-hand fingerings, string numbers, and expression markings. It also includes rhythmic indications, note beaming, and other important details. It is critical to pay attention to this information so that your interpretations will be more accurate.

It is highly advantageous to improve one's notational reading skills, while simultaneously improving technique. Therefore, if possible, it is recommended that the reader use the tablature as a supplement to the standard notation, rather than the main method of learning the notes.

Part I:
Licks and Musical Passages

Dionisio Aguado

Study in E minor

Excerpt: Sextuplet arpeggios

Technical Notes

Break the pattern into two groups:

1. p-i-m

2. a-m-i

Practice the ascending **p-i-m** arpeggio slowly and evenly, using very small motions and quick attacks. Start with a full plant (plant *i*, *m*, and *a* at the same time immediately after *p* plays), then progress to sequential planting (*i* plants after *p* plays, *m* plants after *i* plays, etc.), as this allows the notes to sustain and suits the piece better. For the descending **a-m-i** arpeggio, plant the right-hand fingers sequentially only. Once you feel comfortable practicing each arpeggio separately, play the complete sextuplet pattern while gradually increasing speed. Try to feel the sextuplet arpeggio as one gesture.

The downbeat of measure 8 requires a difficult stretch for the left hand. If you have a hard time reaching the F♯ (4th string) with the 4th finger while keeping your 3rd finger on the high F♯ (1st string), try pivoting on the 2nd finger (which stays on the A on the 3rd string) and playing the F♯ on the 1st string with the 1st finger. Revert back to the original fingering (3rd finger on the F♯ on the 1st string) for the next sextuplet. Make sure not to sustain the notes of the main melody (notes with the stems down) for more than their written duration; otherwise, the separate lines will sound cluttered and unclear.

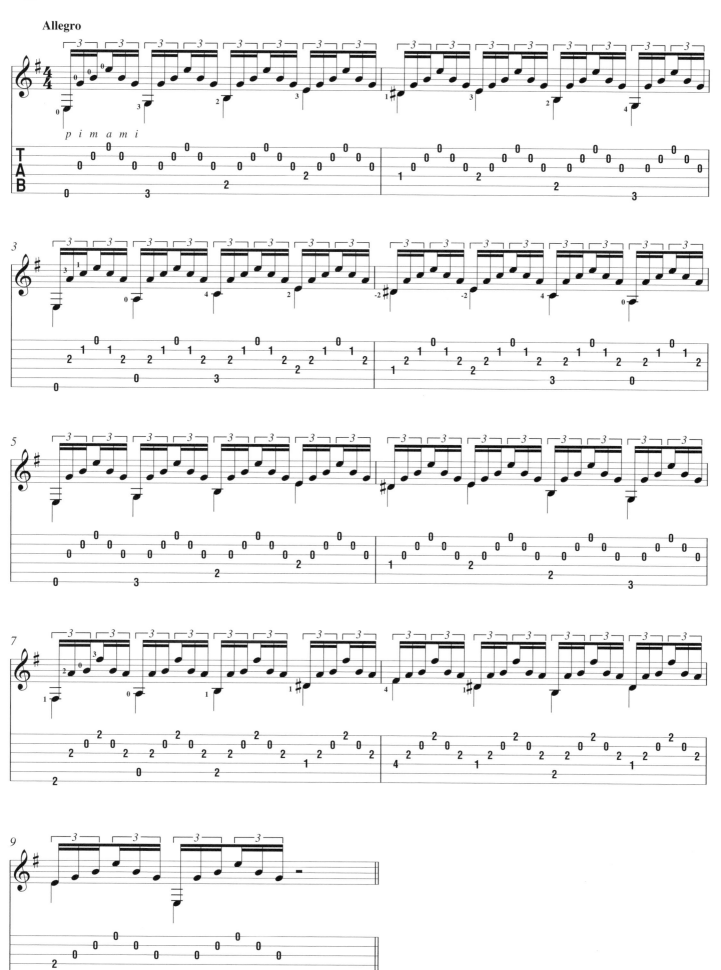

Rondo in A minor, Op. 2, No. 3

Excerpt: Quick successive right-hand finger repetition and stretching

Technical Notes

This excerpt requires the right-hand thumb (measures 1–8) and *i* and *a* (measures 9–12) to play a quick succession of sixteenth notes. During the repeated sixteenth notes, the main melody appears in the alternate voice. Repeating notes successively with one finger (or the thumb) at a fast speed requires very small motions. Keep your right hand steady, making sure that it is not bouncing up and down. It is also important to release the tension as you are playing; otherwise, you will be more likely to stiffen the fingers and make a mistake.

In measure 3, use your 1st finger for the E on the 2nd string and your 4th finger for the C on the 1st string. Try to keep a similar timbre when switching strings. Observe the sixteenth rests that occur in measures 9 and 11 by planting your thumb on the 5th string on the second beat of measure 9 and lifting your left-hand 1st finger on the second beat in measure 11. For the last measure, arpeggiate the chord with a ritardando.

Allegro Moderato

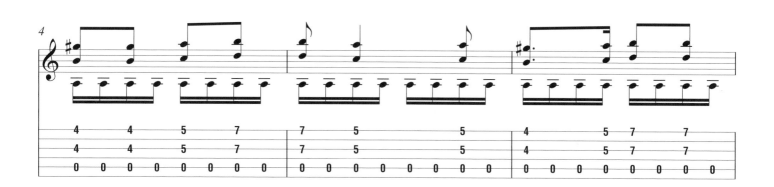

Isaac Albéniz

Asturias (Leyenda)

Excerpt 1: Arpeggios and melodic connectivity

Technical Notes

"Leyenda" begins with an E pedal (measures 1–8) and then moves to a B pedal in measures 9–16. Even though the E notes on the downbeats of measures 1–8 (5th string, 7th fret) are written as eighth notes, sustain these notes until the 1st finger moves to the 4th string (or right before). Likewise, sustain the B notes on the downbeats of measures 9–11 and 13–15 for longer than their written values. This will make the lines sound more cohesive. In addition, connect the melody line (notes with the stems down), being careful not to lift the left-hand fingers early, which will result in a choppy sound. I recommend using the right-hand pattern *p-i-p-m* in this section. The fingering *p-i-p-i* is another option, but repetition of only two fingers at this tempo is more likely to lead to mistakes.

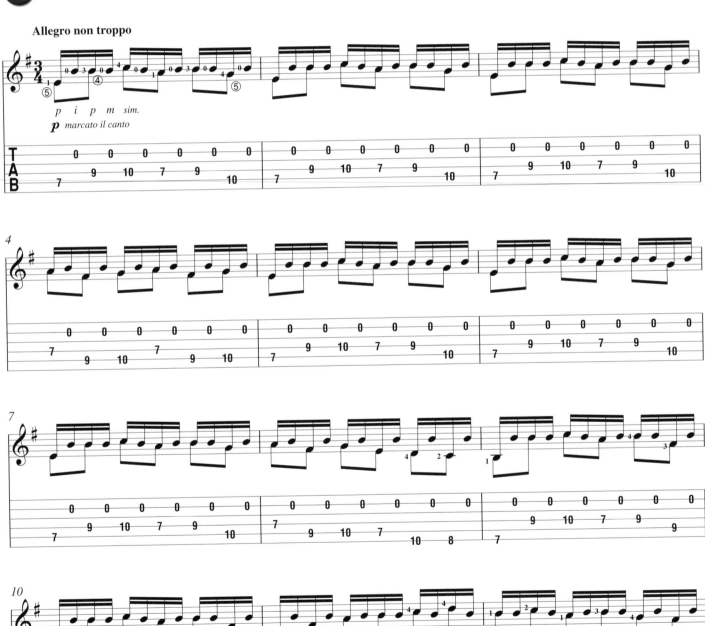

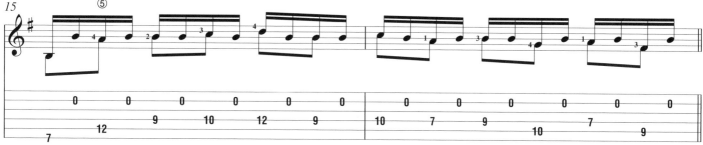

Excerpt 2: Triplet arpeggios on three strings and left-hand stretching

Technical Notes

This excerpt follows the previous example, moving to sixteenth-note triplet arpeggios, or sextuplets. I use the **p-i-a** right-hand pattern for the arpeggios, though **p-i-m** also works well. Practice playing the triplets evenly and clearly, being careful not to play them too quickly, as the lines will become less defined. It is not uncommon to hear musicians play this passage so fast that the definition of the lines becomes blurred.

For more clarity, try moving your right hand towards the bridge (but not necessarily ponticello), which will provide a brighter sound and give your attack more bite. It might also be beneficial to angle your right-hand nails more parallel to the strings, achieving more nail surface (and less flesh) against the string.

Sustain the low E note (open 6th string) throughout measures 1–7, but lift the E (octave above) on the 5th string, 7th fret to help maneuver your 1st finger to the B (3rd string, 4th fret). Avoid using open strings on the main melodic line (notes with the stems down), as the fretted notes will provide a more consistent timbre. For example, I recommend playing the G notes in the melody (e.g., 1st measure, last melody note) on the 4th string, 5th fret instead of the open 3rd string. This requires more stretching, so try to keep your hand loose. If your left-hand thumb tenses up for the stretch at the end of measure 8, you are probably applying more pressure than necessary on the back of the neck. Try momentarily releasing the thumb off the back of the neck.

Allegro

Excerpt 3: Barring and triplet arpeggios on two strings

Technical Notes

Use either your index or middle finger to strum the B major chord at the beginning of each measure. Using your thumb to strum the chords would require a much larger motion to get back into position.

Be careful not to over-extend the motion of the chord strum or it might be hard to move back into position for the next grouping of notes. Keep the rhythm steady and avoid the use of rubato in this section, as it would ruin the forward rhythmic momentum that has been building up to this point. When playing the triplets, practice planting the *m* and *i* fingers in a staccato fashion. Once you perform it at tempo, these staccato notes won't sound out of place.

9

Rumores de la Caleta (Malagueña)

Excerpt: Ascending and descending slurs, arpeggios, and stretching

Technical Notes

In the 2nd measure, bring your left-hand wrist outwards to help facilitate the stretch of the 4th finger to the 5th fret while holding the F and A accompaniment notes on the 3rd and 4th strings. In measure 6, dampen the low E note from the previous measure with the back of the right-hand thumb when plucking the A note on the 5th string. You can play the downbeats of each triplet slur solely with your right-hand thumb or use the ***p-i-m*** combination written. Aim for clarity and evenness when playing the slurs, making them sound similar to the plucked notes.

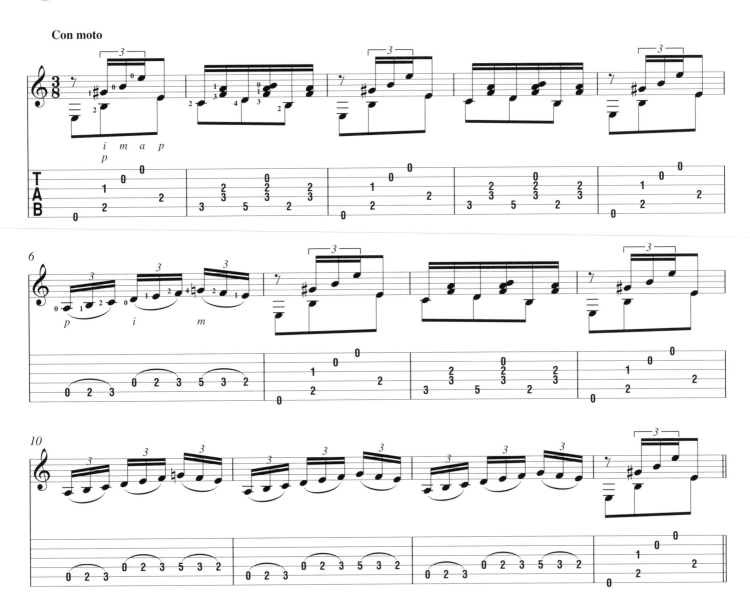

Johann Sebastian Bach

Fugue from Prelude, Fugue, and Allegro, BWV 998

Excerpt 1: Counterpoint, shifting, and string dampening

Technical Notes

(The 6th string is tuned down to D.)

This passage from the Fugue (BWV 998) was originally written in the key of E♭ major but is commonly transposed to D major for the guitar. It requires control of numerous elements to play effectively. In addition to quick shifting, the specific note durations and rests among the multiple lines of counterpoint need to be carefully observed.

One example of a particular shift requiring attention is in the 1st measure. The low G note (3rd beat quarter note) should be held for its full duration and then connected to the following F♯ (4th beat). This requires your left hand to shift from the 1st finger at fret 5 to your 3rd finger at fret 4. Since your 3rd finger is free beforehand, position it as close as possible to the 4th fret, minimizing the motion between the two notes. Although it might not feel natural to position it this way, since your 1st finger is on the 5th fret, this will allow the line to sound more connected and coherent. Try to incorporate this approach throughout the excerpt, thinking ahead and preparing your fingers before they have to shift, if at all possible.

On beats 2 and 4 throughout this excerpt, dampen the previous sustaining notes in the upper line. For example, in the 2nd measure (second eighth-note dyad), dampen the G♯ and E on beat 2 (where the G♯ in the bass is played) by lifting the 1st finger off the G♯ and dampening the open E with the right hand. If you get unwanted sounds by lifting your left hand, try dampening the notes with your right-hand fingers only. For this example, place *i* on the 3rd string in addition to *a* on the 1st string. This should provide a clean way to dampen the notes.

Drop D tuning:
(low to high) D-A-D-G-B-E

Moderato

Excerpt 2: Full and hinge barring, counterpoint, shifting, and note connectivity

Technical Notes

(The 6th string is tuned down to D.)

This is a perfect example of how tricky it can be to hold notes for their written duration while preparing to move to the next note. Preparation and finger placement are paramount if you don't want the lines to sound too detached when shifting. Many of the movements might seem somewhat disjunctive in feel, but keep your left hand as relaxed as possible. This will help keep fatigue to a minimum.

You can also make use of the full barre and the hinge barre to minimize shifting and help connect the lines. For example, in the 1st measure, use a hinge barre with your 1st finger for the F♯ (first quarter note), followed by a partial barre with your 1st finger for the following B note (5th string).

Drop D tuning:
(low to high) D-A-D-G-B-E

Prelude from the 4th Lute Suite, BWV 1006a

Excerpt 1: Scales, string dampening, and shifting

Technical Notes

This is one of Bach's most frequently played pieces on guitar. The Prelude from the 4th Lute Suite is technically demanding and beautiful at the same time. This particular excerpt requires playing quick scales while dampening notes simultaneously and large position shifts. There is a multitude of fingering possibilities for both hands in this piece, so you are encouraged to experiment in this regard.

In the 3rd measure, make sure to dampen the low E note on the 2nd beat. If you use your right-hand thumb to pluck the G♯ (2nd beat, 4th string), try muting the low E string by using your left-hand 2nd finger, which is free at the time. Another option is to use your right-hand thumb to dampen the string if you use an alternate finger to pluck the G♯.

In measure 4, don't let all the notes sustain throughout the entire measure. Instead, lift each finger after the sixteenth-note duration. After plucking an open string, flatten the finger of the following note, so it dampens the ringing open string. For example, the open E on the 1st string (second sixteenth note) can be muted with the 1st finger when you play the subsequent D♯ note on the 2nd string. Also try to keep a consistent tone in the right hand. This is especially important when there are open strings next to fretted notes, which could easily create an uneven timbre if not controlled properly.

Start off with a comfortable tempo on your metronome. Practice playing staccato—planting and preparing each finger—as this is the fastest way to build up speed. It will sound detached when you practice in this fashion, but this will change once you increase the tempo. Make sure to maintain a good, full tone even as you increase the tempo. Pay special attention to your sound since most guitarists produce a thinner timbre when playing fast. If a particular shift or measure is giving you a problem, isolate the area and work on it slowly. Then put all the pieces together while building up your tempo.

Allegro

Excerpt 2: Campanella and position shifting

Technical Notes

You will use the campanella (cross-string) technique for this excerpt. Try to get your tone as even as you can within the three-string pattern, which includes the open E string. The line should be flowing and smooth without gaps when shifting to a new position. Experiment with your right-hand colorations, from ponticello to tasto, to help shape the musical lines. Once again, feel free to experiment with different fingerings, as there are numerous possibilities. In the 1st measure, use your left-hand 1st finger to dampen the low E (beat 2) or your right-hand thumb.

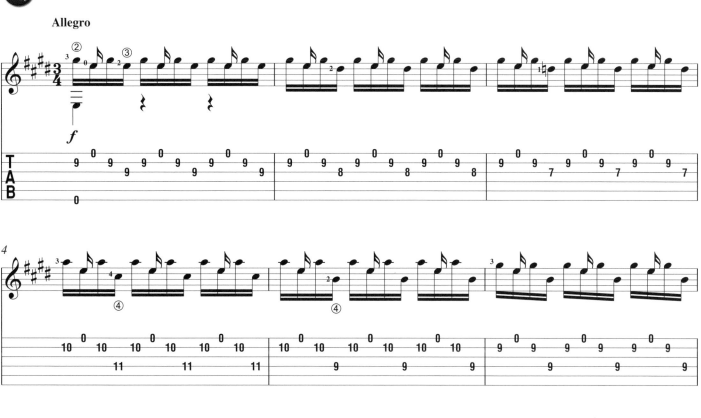

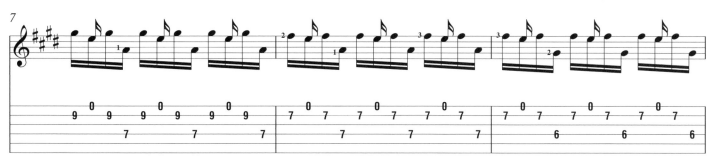

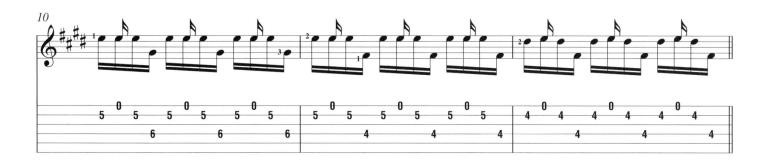

Prelude from the 1st Cello Suite, BWV 1007

Excerpt: Scales and slurs

Technical Notes

(The 6th string is tuned down to D.)

The original key for this suite is G major, and it is most commonly transposed to D major for the guitar. Since this was originally written for cello, I would darken my tone to imitate the mellowness of a cello. Try to connect the lines in a flowing manner, being careful not to articulate the lines in a staccato fashion. Your slurs should produce a sound similar to the plucked notes. Use your ear to adjust how much "snap" your pull-offs produce.

When exploring the right-hand fingering possibilities, I would suggest a combination of all fingers—not just *i* and *m*. If you find that your *a* finger is too bright in timbre compared to the others, adjust the angle (or shape of nail) so that you get more flesh when attacking the string. In measure 6, try dampening the open E (1st string, second sixteenth note) when playing the following C♯ note by flattening your 3rd finger. This dampening technique should be used throughout the passage to help control undesired notes from ringing.

Drop D tuning:
(low to high) D-A-D-G-B-E

Andantino

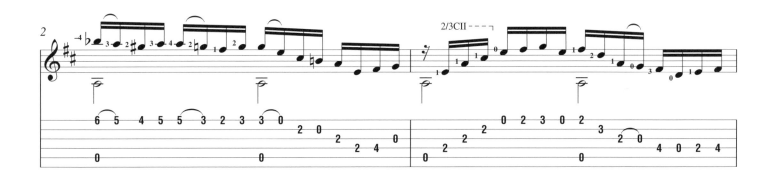

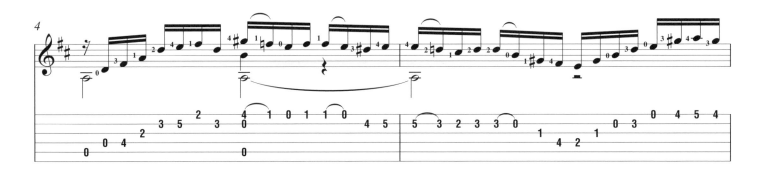

16

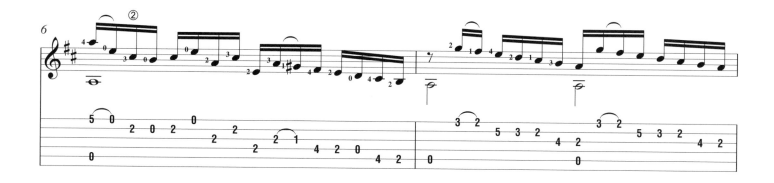

Agustín Barrios Mangoré

Las Abejas

Excerpt: Scales, slurs, and arpeggios

Technical Notes

This piece definitely requires some virtuosity, as it features large shifts, quick scales, slurs, arpeggios, and right-hand string crossing. I have included most right- and left-hand fingerings, but feel free to modify them to your own taste. For example, measure 15 can easily be transformed into cross-string lines, using open strings to help shift from one position to the next.

When there are slurs within a barrage of scalar lines and arpeggios, be sure to articulate your hammer-ons and pull-offs more than usual. If your plucked notes are heavily articulated and your slurs are light, there will be an undesired emphasis on certain notes. By balancing your articulations, your phrasing will have more continuity and flow.

Allegro brillante

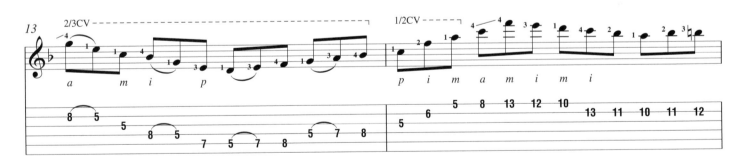

La Catedral (3rd movement)

Excerpt 1: Ascending slurs with arpeggios

Technical Notes

For the right-hand fingering, try using the pattern ***p-i-p-i-p-i-p-a-p-m-i***. Practice it slowly until it feels comfortable, and then gradually increase the speed. Let the notes ring through each arpeggio, being careful not to dampen notes by accident. Connect the last note of each measure to the first note of the following measure. Aim to make the hammer-ons sound similar in attack to the plucked notes to maintain a consistent texture. Lastly, be careful of excess left-hand shifting noises. Either shift just below the callus of your finger where the flesh is softer, or quickly lift your finger vertically when shifting to help minimize noise. If you decide to lift your finger to reduce fret noise, make sure your movement is very fast, so the line doesn't sound disconnected.

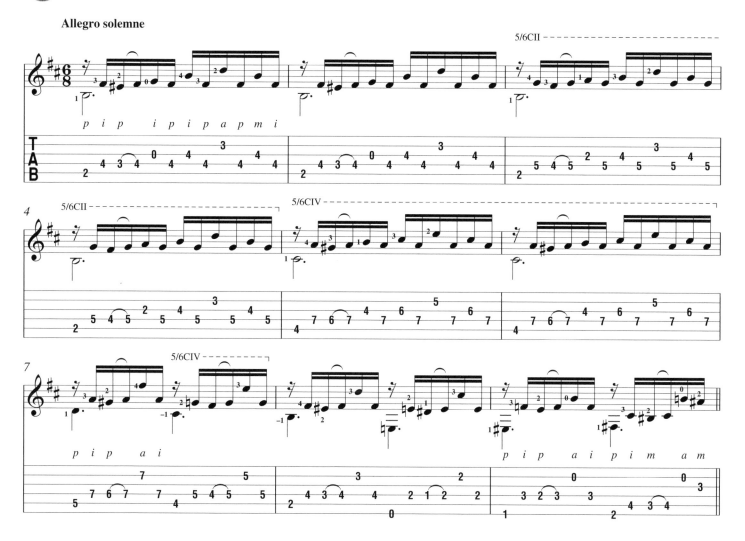

Excerpt 2: Slurs, scale lines, arpeggios, and large position shifts

Technical Notes

There are numerous options for left- and right-hand fingering in this excerpt. I have included some possibilities, but try your own variations to see which ones work best for you. This excerpt contains large position shifts, which must be executed quickly. I would isolate the beginning (before you shift) and the end (after you shift), practicing each part separately, instead of playing the entire phrase over and over. This will allow you to save time and make your practice sessions more productive. In this example, most large shifts have a preceding open string, so use those notes to aid your movement into the new position.

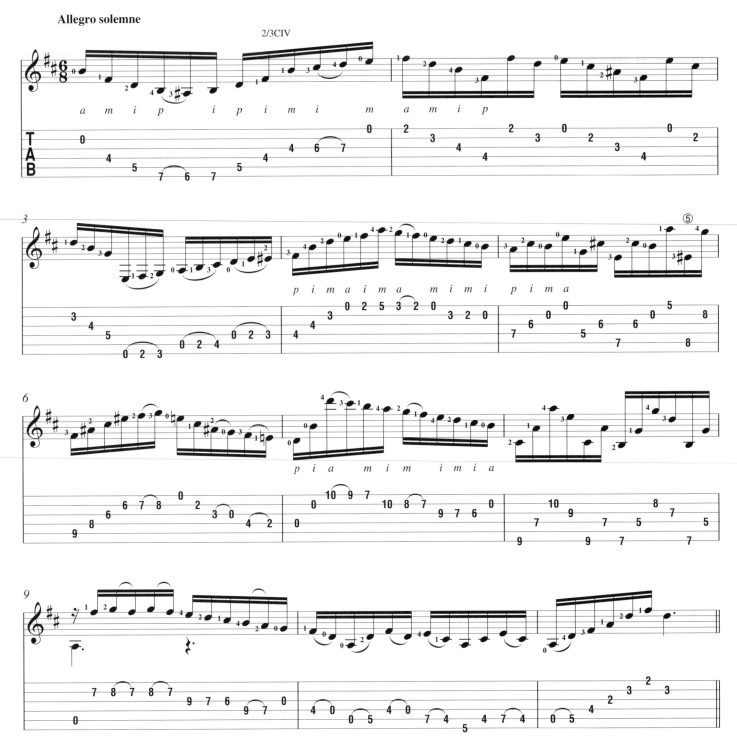

Excerpt 3: Full, hinge, and half barring with arpeggios

Technical Notes

This excerpt is challenging for the left hand, as it contains extended periods of barring, which can lead to fatigue. Although hinge barres can't be used throughout, take advantage of them when you can so that you apply only the absolute minimum pressure needed. For example, in the 1st measure, use the hinge to apply pressure on the 4th and 5th strings instead of the full barre. Also practice quickly releasing the tension of your left hand between each position change to help build endurance.

Allegro solemne

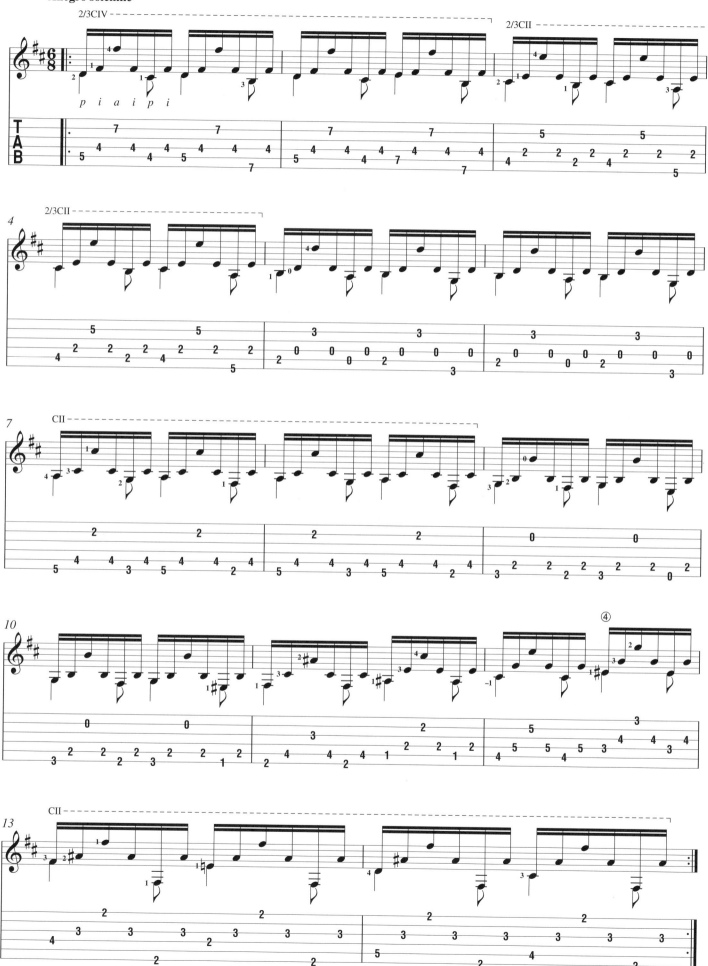

Maxixe

Excerpt: Slurs, arpeggios, and large position shifts

Technical Notes

In the 1st measure, use the open E string to shift to the 2nd position, as this will help make the melodic line sound seamless. Don't apply pressure for the half barre until the C♯ sounds at the end of the measure; it's always best to keep your left hand relaxed until pressure must be applied to sound a note. Try to maintain a flowing quality throughout the excerpt, avoiding a disjointed sound with breaks at the end of phrases. If a left-hand shift is tough to execute in time, practice it slowly until you achieve the desired speed. Maintain a steady tempo and don't use rubato simply because you have difficulty playing the passage in time. Rubato should only be used for musical reasons.

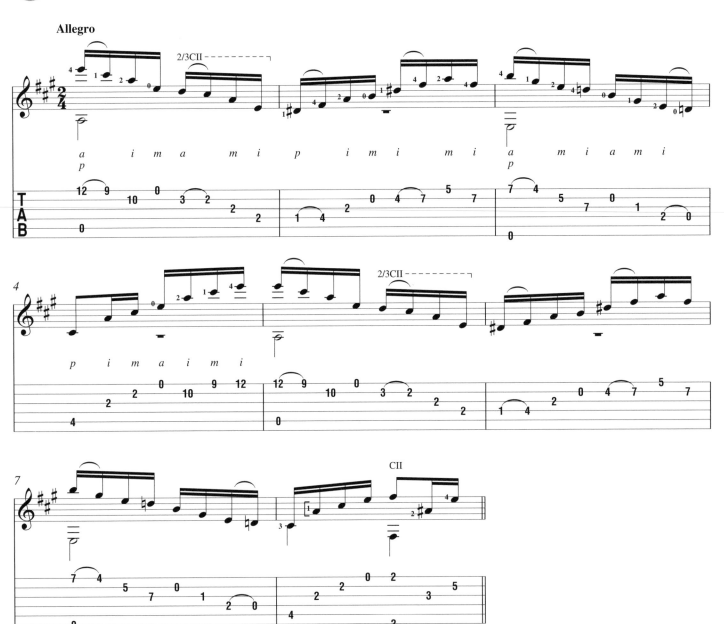

Matteo Carcassi

Study in A minor, Op. 60, No. 7

Excerpt: Tremolo, arpeggios, and slurs

Technical Notes

This is a popular study that features a wide range of techniques, including tremolo (*p-a-m-i*). In measure 6, aim for evenness (over speed) and practice getting your *a-m-i* fingers to sound equal in volume and timbre. The pull-offs in measures 1 to 4 should be clean and sound similar to plucked notes. In measure 7, the transition between the second and third sixteenth-note groupings should be quick and seamless. That means the 2nd finger needs to move in a parallel motion from the 3rd to 4th string in a sixteenth-note succession. In measure 8, I suggest using the hinge barre for the F and B♭ instead of the half barre to help conserve energy.

Allegro

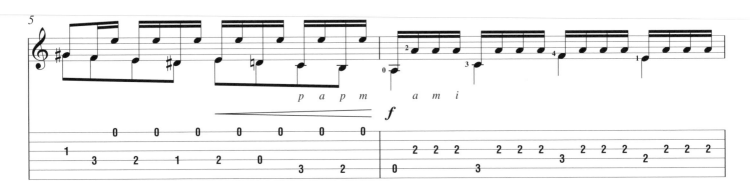

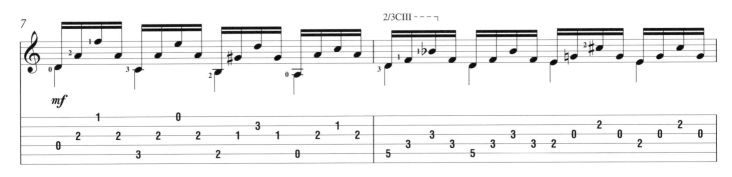

24

François Couperin

Les Barricades Mistérieuses (The Mysterious Barricades)

Excerpt: Counterpoint with suspensions and line connectivity

Technical Notes

This excerpt is taken from the second couplet of this popular rondeau, which was originally written for harpsichord but has been frequently transcribed for the guitar. The original key is B♭, but it is commonly transposed to C for the guitar.

This passage requires some quick movements to keep the suspensions ringing through. At the end of the 2nd measure, the A note can be played with the 3rd finger, but it will require a quick, sudden shift to the following E note on the 4th string. If that is problematic for you, another fingering possibility is to use your 4th finger for the A, which would leave your 3rd finger free for the E note. This fingering would also make the shift to the barre at the beginning of measure 3 more involved, since it would be harder to prepare the 1st finger. Try out both fingerings and see what works best for you.

In measure 3, pay special attention to the shift from the F (second eighth note) to the following A on the 1st string. These notes should not sound too detached, even though the shift is somewhat tricky. Practice preparing the 3rd finger ahead of time for the shift to the A note. Be aware there might be a small gap because of the difficulty, but try to minimize it. In measure 6, use a hinge barre with your 1st finger for the F on the 1st string. It is not necessary to apply pressure to a full barre.

The trill in the last measure is between the upper auxiliary note C and the written B. It can be performed solely on the 2nd string using slurs or by using a cross-string ornamentation on the 2nd and 3rd strings (as written). For the cross-string trill, use the right-hand pattern *a-i-m-i*. If you prefer the slur on the same string, re-finger the last note of the previous measure with the 2nd finger, and use the 3rd finger on the bass note G in the last measure.

Vivement

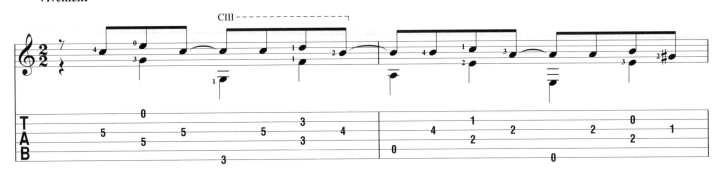

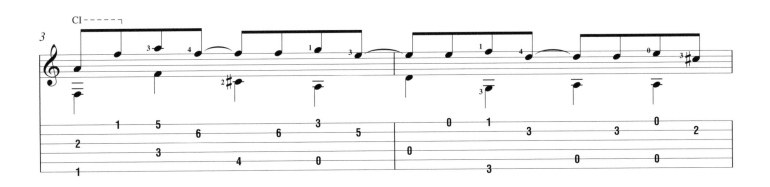

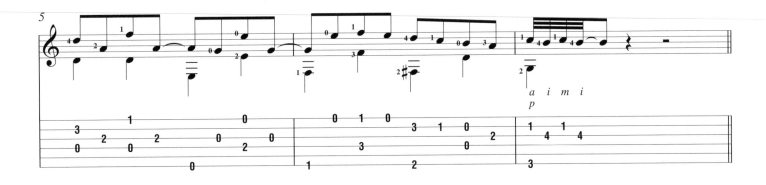

Mauro Giuliani

Grande Ouverture, Op. 61

Excerpt 1: Scales, arpeggios, and slurs

Technical Notes

The Grande Ouverture is one of the well-known tour de force pieces within the classical guitar repertoire. It contains many virtuosic techniques and additionally requires high endurance, with long passages of quick repetitions. For this first passage, start off practicing the lines slowly in a staccato fashion, increasing your speed incrementally. Your slurs should have a similar articulation to the plucked notes. Keep motions in both hands to a minimum, as there are many quick shifts.

In measure 7, make sure your right hand isn't positioned too close to the bridge, since this could result in an overly bright and harsh tone. Whenever you are playing on the treble strings at a forte dynamic level (or louder), bright timbres can become overdone quite easily, so right-hand positioning should be carefully thought out. In measure 8, the penultimate note B (5th string) should be played with your 2nd finger, since it will make the transition to the A chord in the next measure much easier than using the 1st finger. (Using the 1st finger would require a parallel motion to the 2nd and 3rd strings, which is a tougher shift to do quickly.)

Allegro maestoso

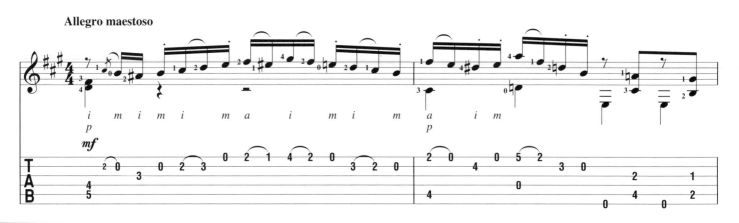

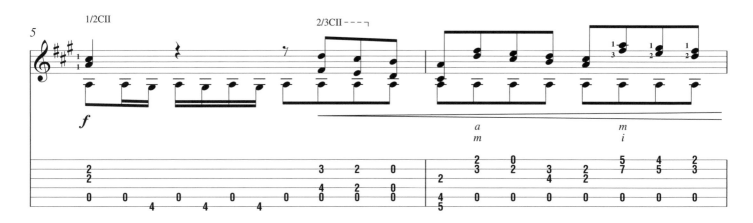

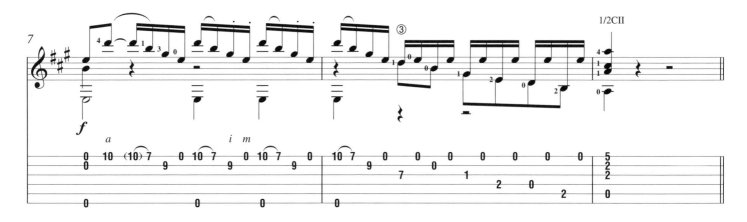

Excerpt 2: Ascending and descending triplet arpeggios

Technical Notes

For the sixteenth-note triplets, use the ***m-i-p*** pattern with the right hand. If your right hand starts feeling fatigued, consider changing to ***a-i-p*** from measure 9 through the first triplet of measure 11. In passages featuring fast repeated patterns with the right hand, it is important to have different fingering options to help keep your right hand as relaxed as possible.

The melody moves to the bass in measures 4–8 and 12–17. These notes should be accented, but make sure that the remaining notes of each triplet are articulated and defined. If you find that your thumb is not producing enough sound, pluck the thumb notes at an angle (more into the soundboard), so that it is closer to a rest stroke. I don't recommend the use of a full rest stroke, which would result in an overly boomy sound compared to the *i* and *m* fingers, which are playing free strokes on the 2nd and 1st strings.

Allegro

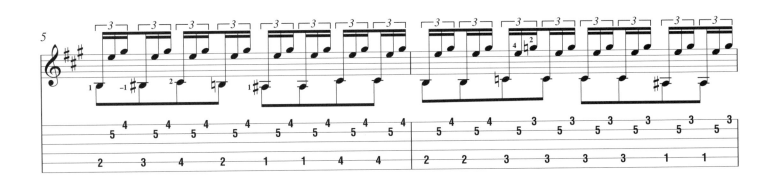

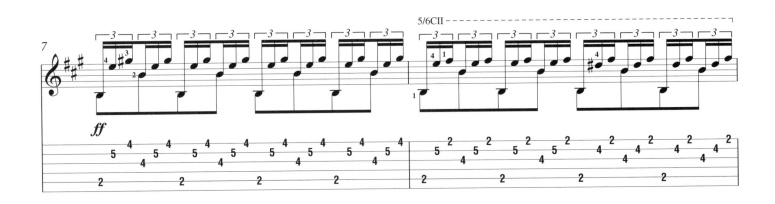

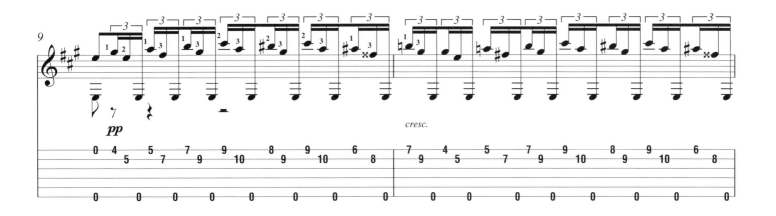

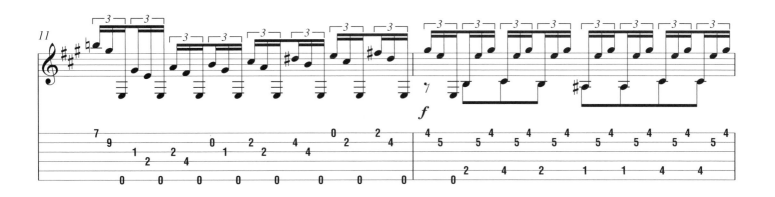

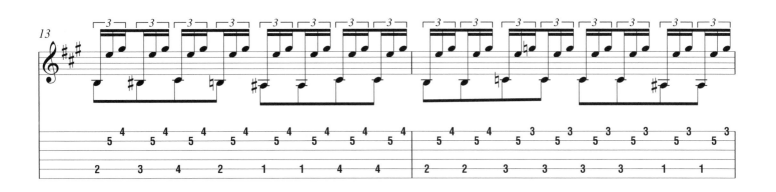

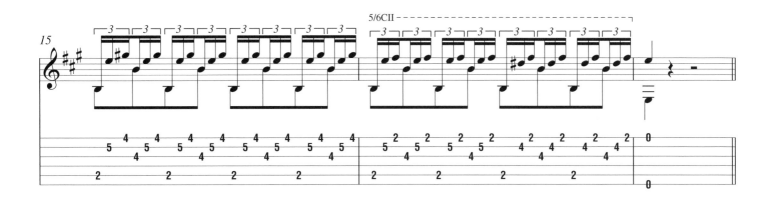

Excerpt 3: Ascending and descending triplet arpeggios with string skipping

Technical Notes

This excerpt is similar to the previous example and features higher position shifts and right-hand string skipping. Measures 1–8 use the descending *m-i-p* arpeggios pattern throughout. Measure 9 requires the right hand to alternate between *a-i-p* and *m-i-p* patterns quickly. Use *a-i-p* when the arpeggios occur on the 1st, 3rd, and 5th strings (e.g., A–C♯–A arpeggio) and *m-i-p* when the arpeggios are on the 1st, 2nd, and 5th strings (e.g., D–F♯–A arpeggio).

Excerpt 4: Octave arpeggios

Technical Notes

For the A octaves near the end of the 1st measure, try using the hinge with your left-hand 2nd finger for the A on the 3rd string, while simultaneously lifting off the preceding E octave on the 4th string. It's also possible to use the 3rd finger to fret the A note, but this makes the transition to the G♯ with the 4th finger more awkward.

Your right hand begins with a repeating *p-i* pattern. When the octaves move to different strings, alternate between *p-i* and *p-m*. Repeating only two fingers requires more up and down right-hand movement, which should be avoided. It also creates a higher probability of making errors. Feel free to experiment with different figurations, including adding the *a* finger into the mix.

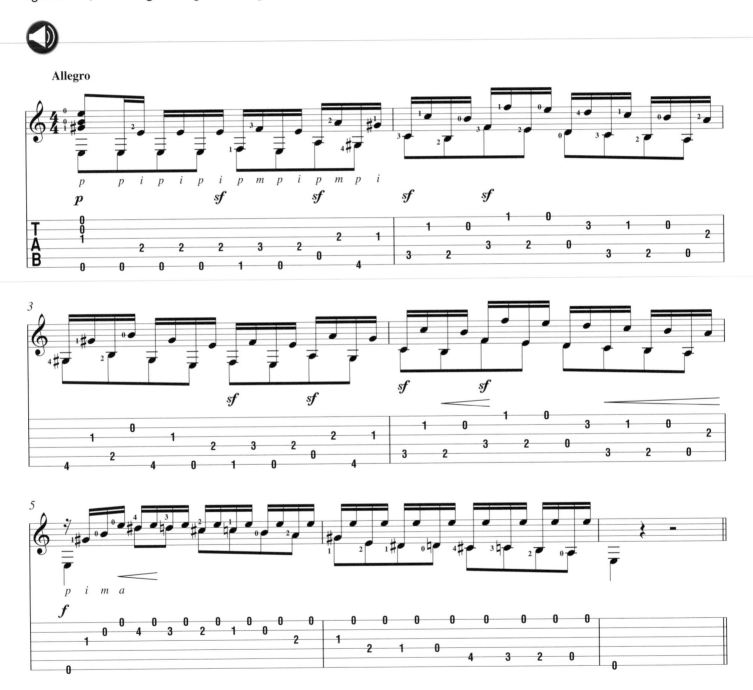

Excerpt 5: Melody/accompaniment, large position shifts, and arpeggios

Technical Notes

In the 1st measure, play the main melody (notes with the stems up) slightly louder than the accompaniment. If you are having difficulty bringing out the melody, try using rest strokes with your *a* finger, though make sure that the rest strokes don't overpower the accompaniment so much that there is a drastic change in timbre. On the 2nd beat of the 3rd measure, use your right-hand thumb to dampen the open A string and use the same dampening technique on the 4th beat to stop the low E. The bass notes in measure 6 can be dampened in the same way, though it is also possible to dampen the bass notes with your left hand. For example, the open A string can be dampened by extending your 1st finger on the 2nd beat.

Allegro

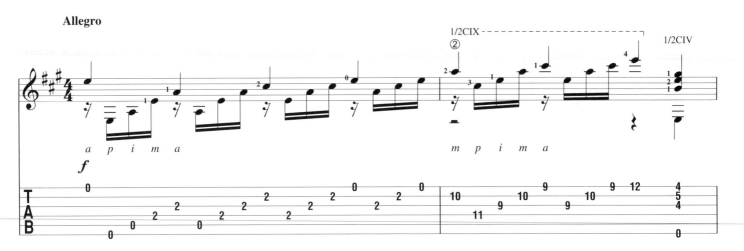

Variations on "Les Folies d'Espagne," Op. 45

Excerpt: Melody/accompaniment and triplet slurs

Technical Notes

This excerpt, from the second variation of the piece, utilizes numerous hammer-ons and pull-offs. Hold the main melody notes (notes with the stems down) for their full duration to create a legato line, but be careful not to hold them beyond their written duration.

Since most guitarists have a difficult time controlling their articulation with left-hand slurs, go slowly at first, recognizing which fingers give you trouble. The 4th finger is usually the most problematic, so pay special attention to measures that feature slurs with that particular finger (e.g., measure 4). Many of the triplet slurs have quick decrescendos, so the attack of the pull-off does not need to be accentuated.

In the transition from measure 5 to 6, I recommend fingering the E on the downbeat of measure 6 with the 2nd finger (instead of the 1st finger) and then slurring the C♯ and D with your 3rd and 4th fingers, respectively. Keep the 3rd finger on the C♯ until the last note of the measure and then switch to the 2nd finger. This fingering will make the transition to the next measure easier.

Andantino

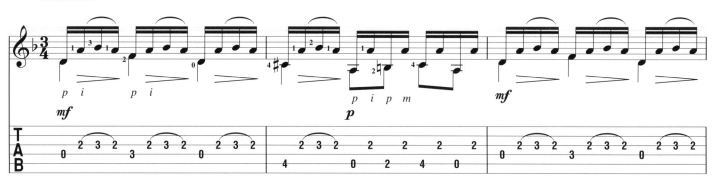

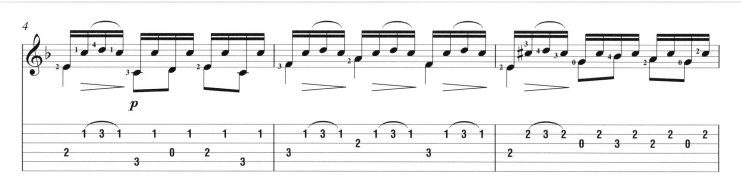

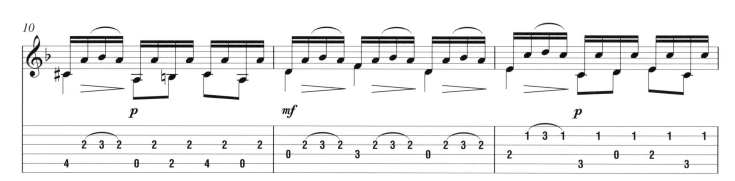

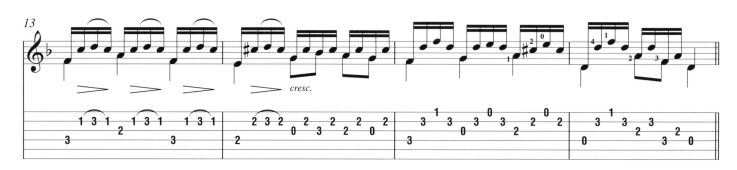

Enrique Granados

Danza Española No. 5

Excerpt 1: Stretching and connectivity of melody

Technical Notes

This work was originally written for the piano and has arguably gained more popularity on the guitar. It features a main melody with accompaniment, and it is important that the melody sings with full rhythmic duration on each note, even if it requires a stretch that is difficult to hold. In measure 5, keep the 4th finger on the high B melody note (2nd string) while the 1st finger holds the B on the 6th string and *i* and *m* play the E and B on the 2nd and 3rd strings, respectively. If you don't have large hands, you might need to extend your left-hand wrist outwards to help facilitate the reach.

Andante – quasi Allegretto

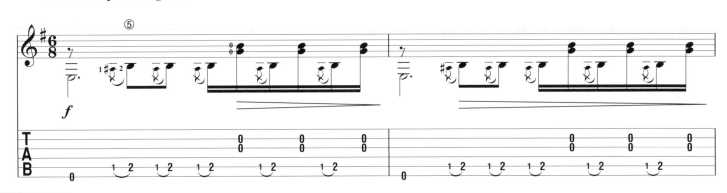

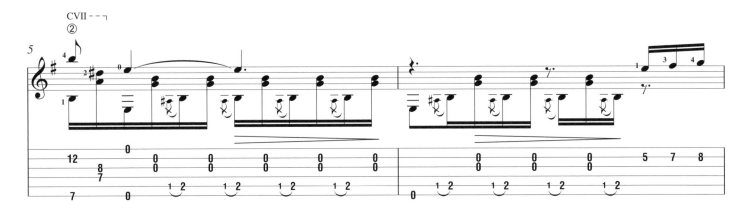

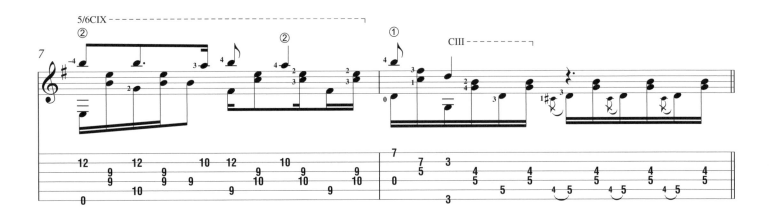

David Kellner

Phantasia in D minor

Excerpt: Campanella and ornaments

Technical Notes

(The 6th string is tuned down to D.)

This piece was originally written for the lute, which has a brighter tone compared to the contemporary guitar. For this reason, try brightening up the timbre of this passage by using more right-hand nail than usual.

The combination of slurs and quick shifts should be practiced in small groups. Once you feel comfortable playing the small groups, combine them together. For example, you could separate the 2nd and 3rd measures into three groups (first group in 3rd position, second group in 2nd position, and third group back in 3rd position) and practice the shifts according to your left-hand position. There are many possibilities for left- and right-hand fingerings in this passage. Make sure your right-hand fingerings do not create unwanted accents and tone colors. This is especially important when using the thumb on the upper strings, as it tends to sound heavier than the other fingers.

For the trill in measure 4, there are two options: slurring the A and G♯ notes on the 3rd string with your 3rd and 1st fingers alternating, or using a cross-string trill. For the cross-string trill, I recommend using *p-m-p-i* with your right-hand fingers, being careful to articulate the notes evenly, as it is easy to overpower the *i* and *m* fingers with the thumb stroke.

Drop D tuning:
(low to high) D-A-D-G-B-E

Rubato

Luigi Legnani

Caprice No. 7

Excerpt 1: Scale bursts

Technical Notes

This excerpt begins with short scale bursts, which are great practice for building speed. The scalar passages in measures 1–4 can be fingered in a number of different ways with the left hand, including playing the entire passage on the top three strings or using only the 2nd and 1st strings. Although both have their own advantages, I wrote out the first fingering option since the entire passage can be played in the 9th position (the other option requires three position shifts). When shifting from chord to chord in measures 5–7, use the softer part of your flesh below the calluses to help reduce string noise.

Three right-hand fingering options are given for the scale bursts in measures 1–4. The first two patterns use *i* and *m* fingers, and the third pattern uses *i*, *m*, and *a* fingers. I would recommend practicing all the variations, as they are commonly used within classical repertoire. As a general rule, you should try to avoid successive finger repetitions in rapid lines. Aim for a light touch (without sounding thin) when playing these passages to suit the character of the music and to provide clarity to the quick lines.

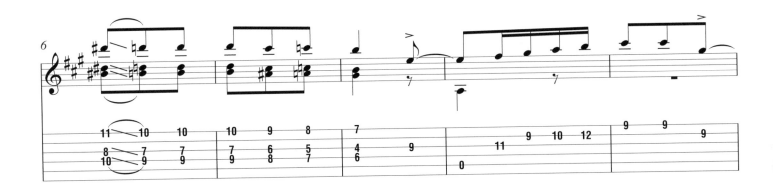

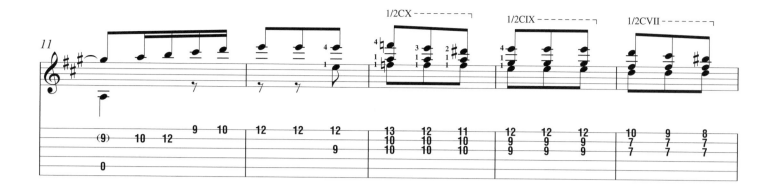

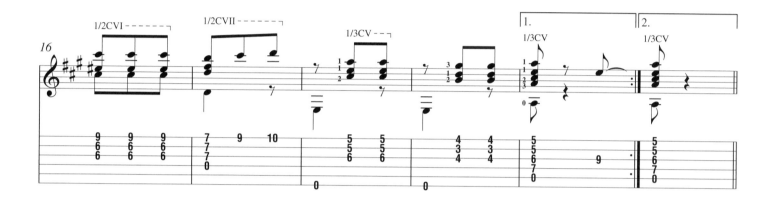

Excerpt 2: Slurs, arpeggios, and quick shifting

Technical Notes

As in the previous example, this virtuosic passage is played at a prestissimo tempo. Make sure the notes are played evenly and clearly and that the slurs sound similar in attack to the plucked notes. The left hand encounters some large leaps, so keep your motions as small as possible to aid in the numerous shifts. In the transition from measure 2 to 3, dampen the open E (6th string) with the back of your thumb while playing the following A (5th string) to avoid a muddy texture. Later in measure 3, lift the half barre when plucking the last sixteenth (open E). When plucking the first note of measure 4, dampen the open E by flattening the 2nd finger (used for the A note).

Caprice No. 15

Excerpt: Arpeggios, slurs, and large position shifts

Technical Notes

Practice this excerpt slowly and play every note staccato. Once you build up the tempo, the musical line won't sound as detached. Be careful to play the bass notes for their written duration; avoid cutting them short or holding them longer than indicated. For example, in measure 1, lift the quarter-note B (on the 5th string) once you pluck the F♯ on the 2nd beat and hold the A♯ in measure 3 for a full quarter note. At the end of the 1st measure, keep your 4th finger close to the fingerboard before and during the shift to the high B note (2nd measure). In measures 9–14, feel free to change the left-hand fingering, since there are many possible variations.

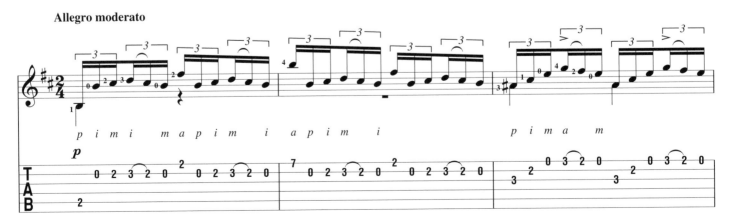

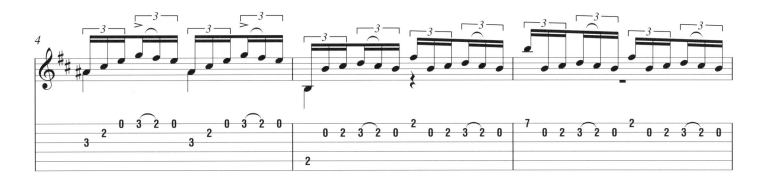

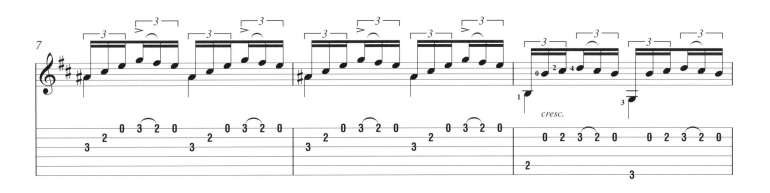

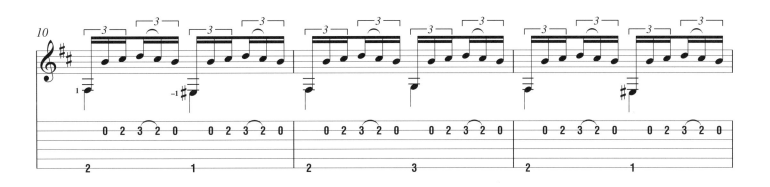

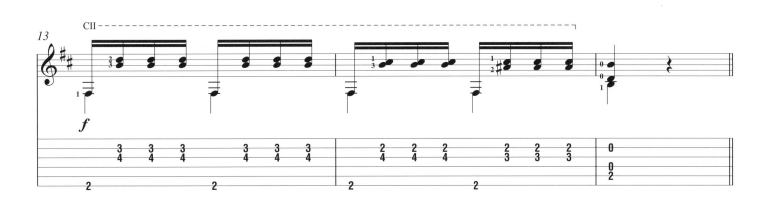

Niccolò Paganini

Caprice No. 24

Excerpt 1: Large position leaps, slurs, and high-register facility

Technical Notes

Originally written for violin, Paganini's 24th Caprice is a popular illustration of virtuosic technique and classical bravado. This excerpt features many position shifts, so any excessive motions in the left hand will make it more difficult to perform. Focus on keeping your left-hand fingers close to the fingerboard. To observe the rests in the bass voice, use your right hand to mute the previously played open strings. The high E note in measure 4 can be played by shifting your 1st finger over from the penultimate note in measure 3 or by using a hinge barre with your 1st finger. Also make sure not to sustain the A note from the previous measure when playing the high E.

Try using a hinge barre in measure 5, 2nd position. If the F♯ on the 1st string accidently sounds when positioning into the hinge barre, an option is to use your 2nd finger for the C♯ on the 2nd string instead and use your 1st finger to produce a hinge barre for the 3rd and 4th strings.

In measure 7, shift to the high G note (15th fret, 1st string) with your 4th finger, while keeping your 1st finger close to the D (10th position, 1st string). When playing this piece at a fast tempo, it will be hard to achieve a clean pull-off if you shift your 1st finger away from the 10th fret. In measures 6 and 7, use a guide finger when shifting quickly on the same string. Cut the 1st note of each shift a little short, so you can hit the subsequent notes in time.

Quasi Presto

Excerpt 2: Natural and artificial harmonics with bass notes

Technical Notes

The 3rd variation of Caprice No. 24 involves plucking a bass line with the thumb while the *i* and *a* fingers play natural and artificial harmonics. Playing artificial harmonics (also called "harp harmonics"—"H.H." in notation) requires the following three steps, which occur simultaneously:

- Left-hand finger is applied

- Right-hand index finger (*i*) touches the string exactly 12 frets higher

- Right-hand annular (*a*) finger plucks the harmonic

For example, in order to play the high C artificial harmonic on the downbeat of measure 1, fret the C note (2nd string, 1st fret) with the left-hand 1st finger, place the tip of the right-hand index finger directly over the 13th fret, and pluck the string with the *a* finger. At the same time, your thumb is plucking the low C (5th string, 3rd fret).

For natural harmonics, such as the E harmonic on the last beat of measure 2, the left hand is not required to fret any note. Simply place the tip of the index finger over the 12th fret of the 1st string and pluck with the *a* finger (while also plucking the E bass note with the thumb).

Once your harmonic technique is comfortable, try to connect the notes as much as possible to make the musical line flow. This will require quick shifting from one note to another. Feel free to modify the fingering if you feel an alternate fingering helps you shift more easily.

Expressivo

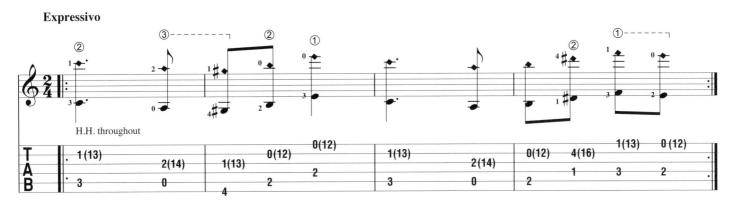

H.H. throughout

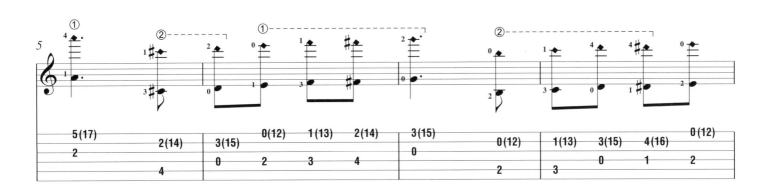

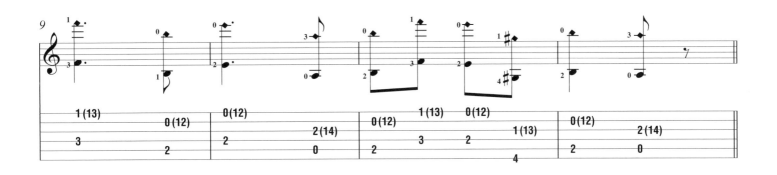

Fernando Sor

Gran Solo, Op. 14

Excerpt: Stretching, slurs, and shifting

Technical Notes

(The 6th string is tuned down to D.)

This excerpt requires some difficult stretches for the left hand. In measures 1–4, extend your 4th finger to the 9th and 10th frets while holding down a half barre on the 5th fret. During the stretches, bring your left-hand wrist out slightly, as this will extend your reach and help minimize any strain, particularly if you have smaller hands. The transition from measure 4 to 5 features a large leap, so isolate the shift and practice it slowly and in a relaxed manner, gradually increasing the speed until there is no gap in the rhythm.

Drop D tuning:
(low to high) D-A-D-G-B-E

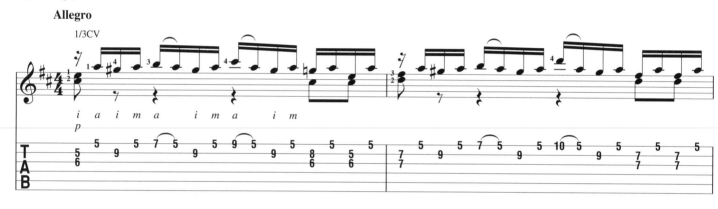

Variations on a Theme of Mozart, Op. 9

Excerpt 1 (Variation 4): Arpeggios, note dampening, and hinge barring

Technical Notes

Be sure to observe the many sixteenth rests throughout the variation. I recommend first trying to dampen the notes with your right hand, as this will allow more time to prepare for the left-hand shifts that follow. If this is too difficult at times, use one of your left-hand fingers to mute any remaining sound. At the beginning of the excerpt, there are many possibilities for right-hand fingering, but I recommend ***a-i-m*** for the triplet, followed by ***p*** and ***i*** for the downbeat of the 1st measure. Make sure you don't accent your thumb too much, as it's easy to overpower your index finger. At the end of measure 7, use a hinge barre for the F♯ on the 1st string to make the transition from the previous note (B on the 5th string) smoother.

Andantino

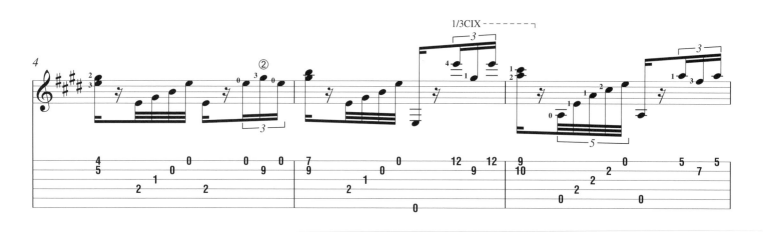

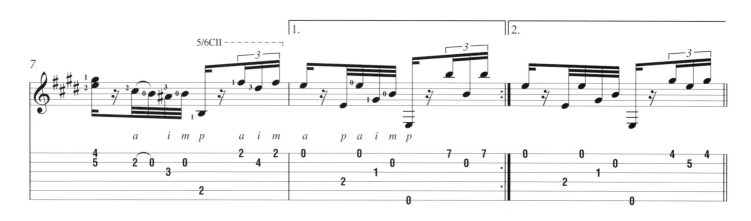

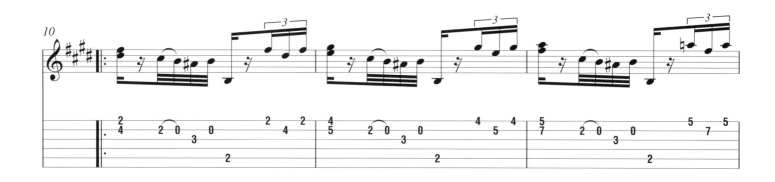

Excerpt 2 (Variation 5): Triplets with slurs, arpeggios, and register changes

Technical Notes

Connect and shape the melody notes, keeping the accompaniment at a slightly lower dynamic level. Practice controlling the loudness of your pull-offs so they don't overpower the melodic line. For instance, in the 1st measure, at the end of the first triplet, the B should not be louder than the G♯ melody note preceding it. Starting in measure 14, pluck the triplets using either *m-p-i* or *i-p-m*. Don't lift your left-hand fingers too quickly, or the resulting sound will be too detached and choppy.

Andantino

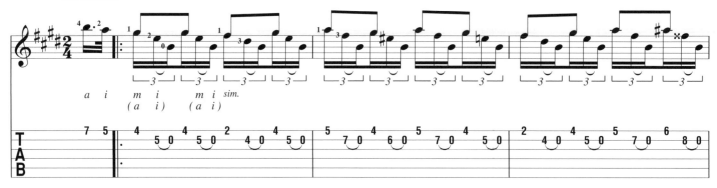

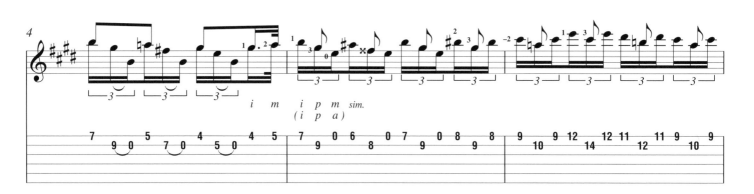

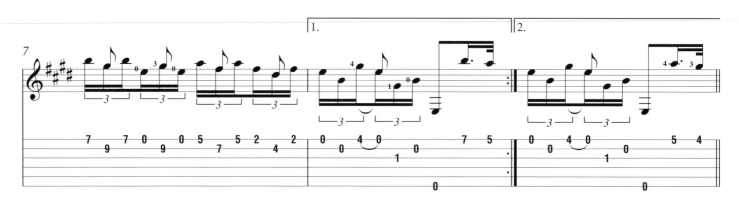

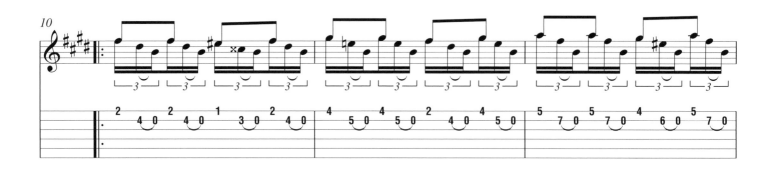

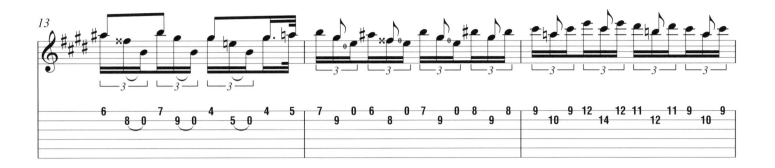

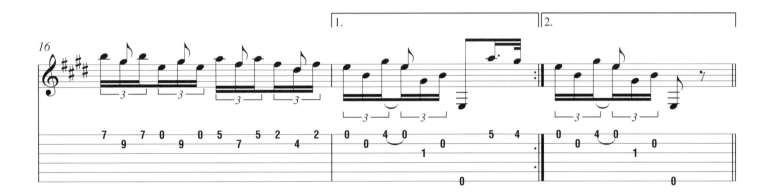

Francisco Tárrega

Capricho Arabe

Excerpt 1: Slurs with quick shifts, scales, and rubato

Technical Notes

(The 6th string is tuned down to D.)

This excerpt begins with a combination of slurs and quick shifting. Practice connecting the last note of each slur grouping to the first note of the next grouping. The shifts must be executed quickly to keep the melodic line flowing and lyrical, but practice them slowly at first and gradually increase the speed. In measure 10, add a portamento between the A and E on the 4th string, maintaining pressure on the string throughout the shift. In the following measure, try playing the passage alternating *i* and *m* and then experiment with different right-hand fingerings (e.g., *m-i*, *i-m-a*, etc.) to see which works best for you. Experiment with the use of rubato in this passage and let the line breathe while keeping it virtuosic.

Drop D tuning:
(low to high) D-A-D-G-B-E

Andantino Rubato

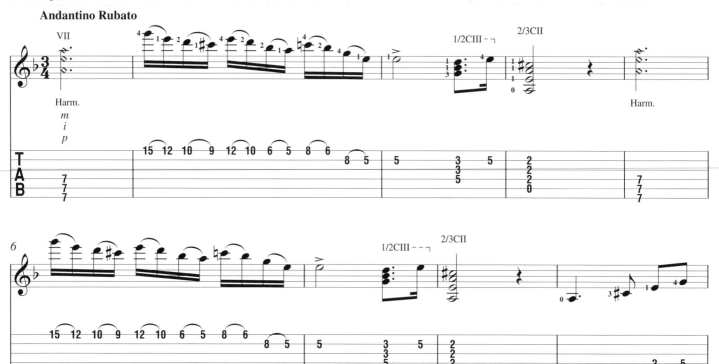

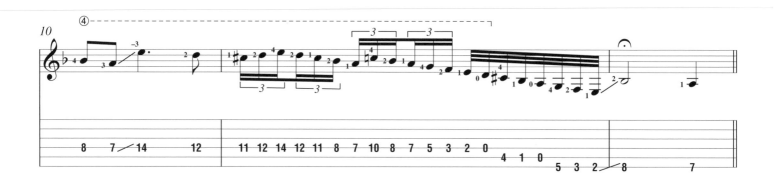

Excerpt 2: High-position slurs and shifting

Technical Notes

(The 6th string is tuned down to D.)

This passage includes more quick shifts with slurs. Isolate any difficult shifts and practice them separately. For example, in measure 2, work on shifting your 2nd finger from the 6th to the 10th fret and from the 10th to the 13th fret. Before shifting, look first at the new position to anticipate exactly how far you have to move your left hand. You don't want to be looking back and forth on the fingerboard more than necessary.

Drop D tuning:
(low to high) D-A-D-G-B-E
Andantino Rubato

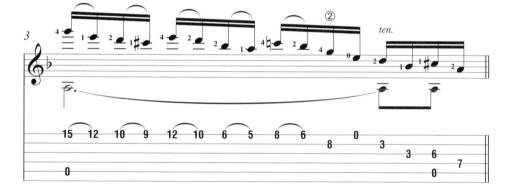

Gran Jota Aragonesa

Excerpt: Snare drum technique

Technical Notes

This piece from the 19th century features one of the most interesting extended guitar techniques. In this passage, you will perform the snare drum technique while playing a melody line on top. Snare drum technique (also known as *tabalet*) is produced by crossing two bass strings (in this case, the 5th and 6th strings) over one another and then plucking the strings with your right hand.

At the beginning of the excerpt, play the snare drum pattern by alternating your index and middle fingers. When the melody enters at the pickup of measure 9, use your thumb to pluck the bass-string snare drum pattern, as *i* and *m* will be needed to pluck the melody. Your left-hand index finger will stay fixed at the 9th position and will be required to barre in numerous spots.

Ad libitum

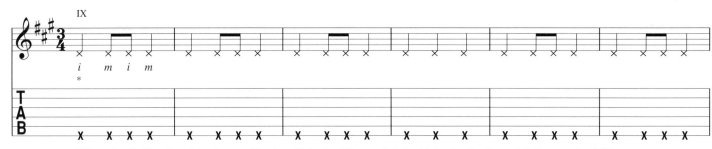

*"Snare drum" effect: Cross 5th string over 6th string with fret-hand finger and pluck with thumb only when melody is present (m. 8–24).

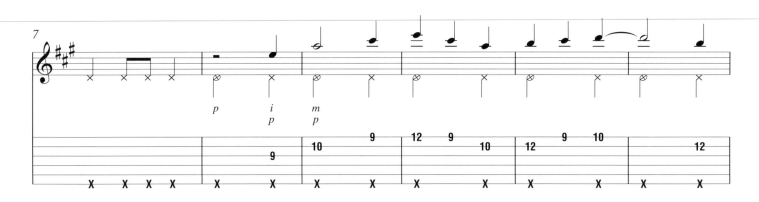

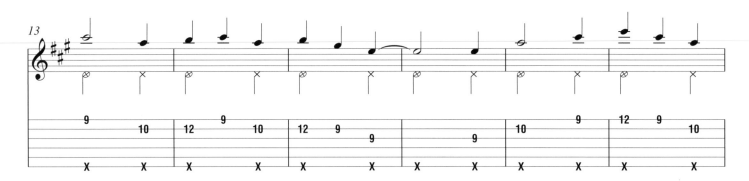

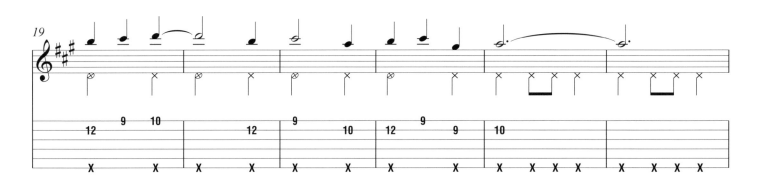

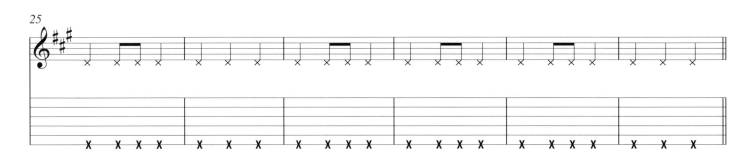

Recuerdos de la Alhambra

Excerpt: Tremolo with large position shifts and triplet slurs

Technical Notes

When practicing this tremolo passage, play the **a-m-i** notes evenly and staccato at a slow tempo. It will sound much smoother once it is played at the full tempo. In measure 4, shift to the 10th position when hitting the open A on the 5th string. Later in the measure, practice isolating the large shift back to the 2nd position so there isn't a gap. Feel free to incorporate the use of rubato into the shift, as it would be musically appropriate. In general, the piece shouldn't be played too metronomically, or its romantic qualities will be diminished.

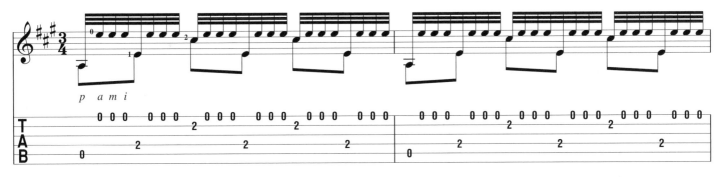

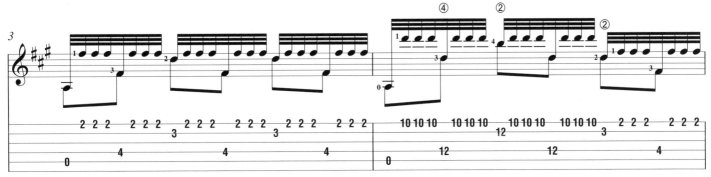

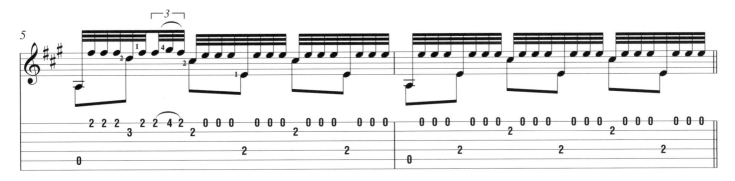

Part II: Historical Exercises

Warm-Up and Technical Workout Exercises

120 Right-Hand Studies (with alternate chord variations)

Mauro Giuliani

The *120 Right-Hand Studies*, from Op.1 by Mauro Giuliani, are some of the most important arpeggio studies for classical guitar. They include a large number of right-hand configurations that one would encounter within the classical guitar literature. There is a wide range of complexity within the right-hand configurations, so I recommend starting with simple patterns, such as 1–10. Once you have already developed some comfort, add new examples incrementally. Practice with a metronome to help keep your rhythm steady. Emphasize good tone production, tension release, clarity of sound, speed development, and endurance.

In addition to practicing these studies as they were originally written, I have also included some alternate chord progressions. These examples give variations in sound and help release tension in the left hand by implementing the 1st and 2nd open strings. It is not uncommon for the left-hand 1st finger to feel tense when performing these studies for long practice sessions. It is important that you are constantly relaxed. If there is pain, take a break! The main point of these studies is to develop your right hand. It is not meant as a left-hand tension exercise. I encourage you to come up with your own chord progressions, as this will ease any repetitious nature that could occur with extended periods of practicing.

Alternate Example #1

Alternate Example #2

Original

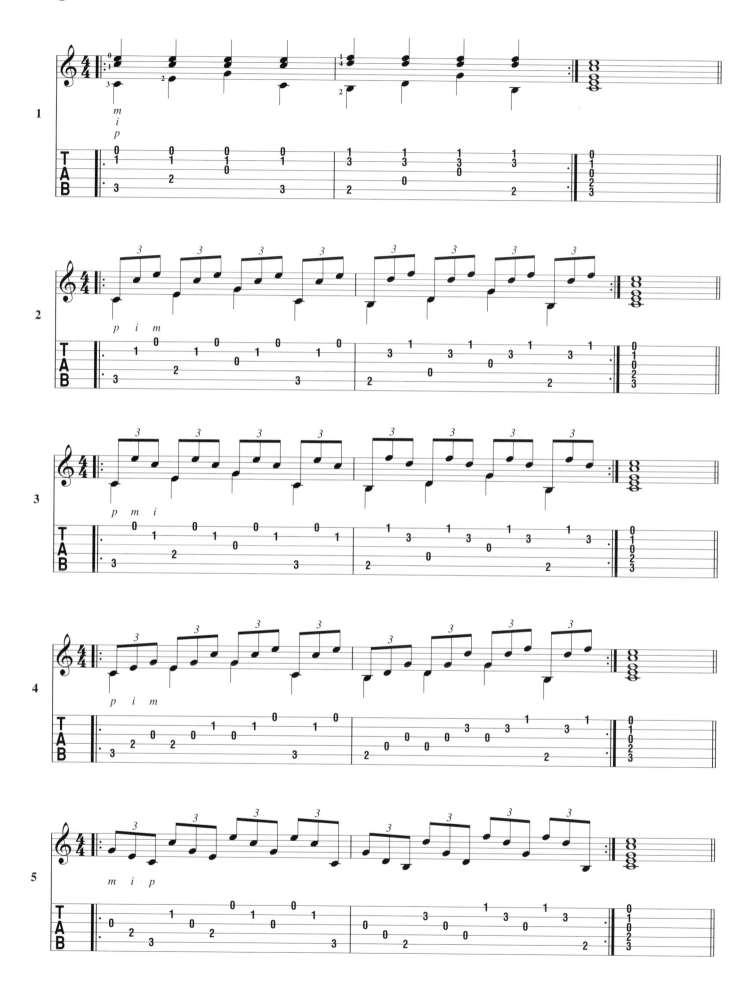

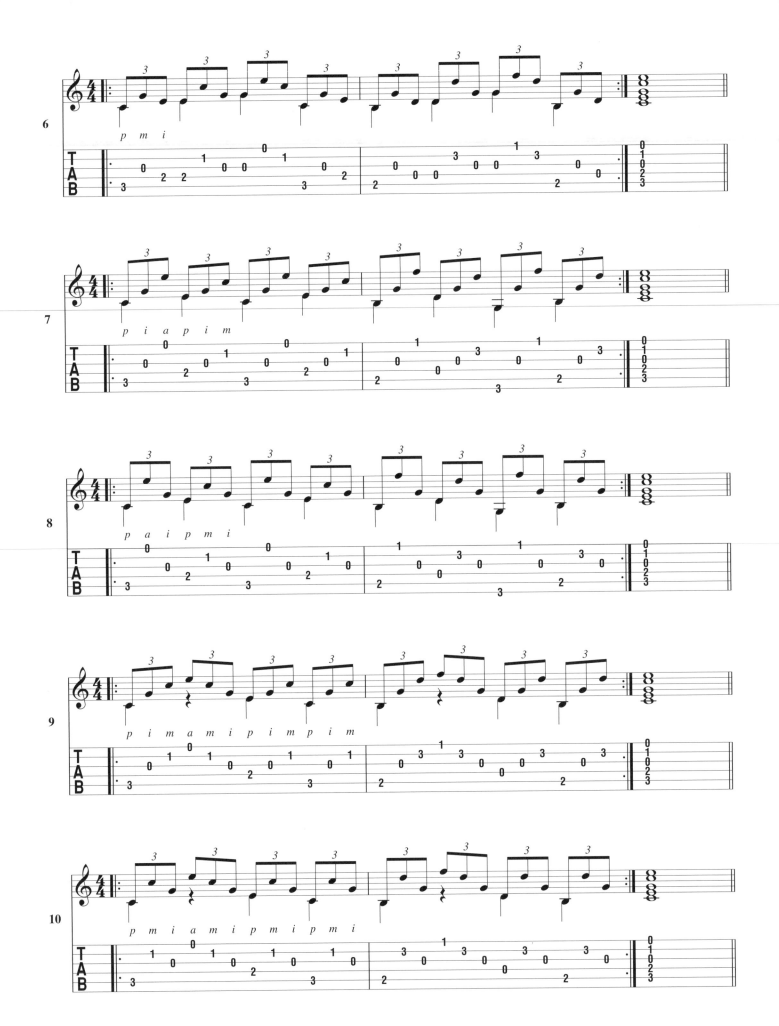

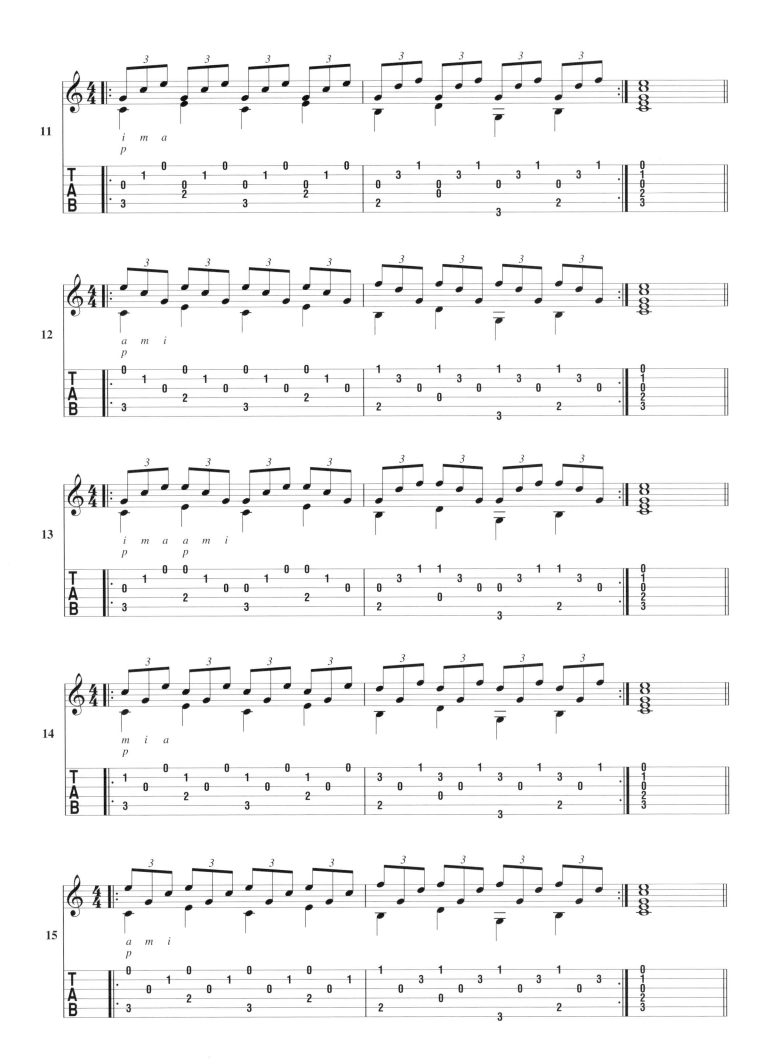

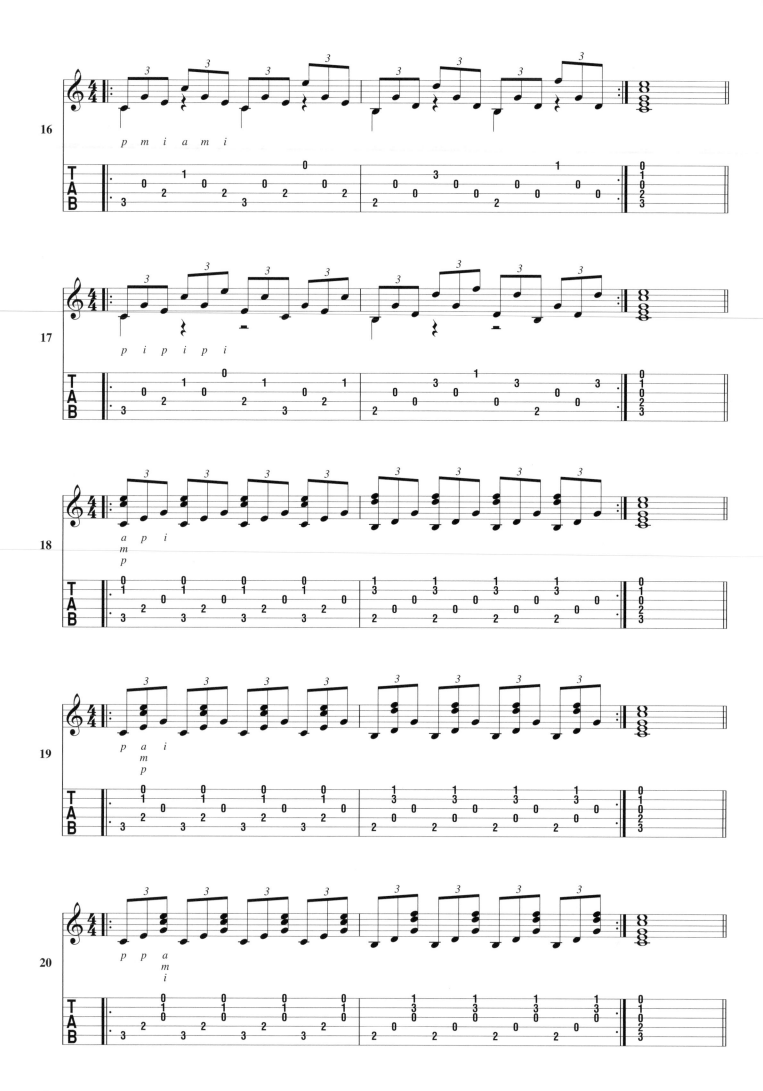

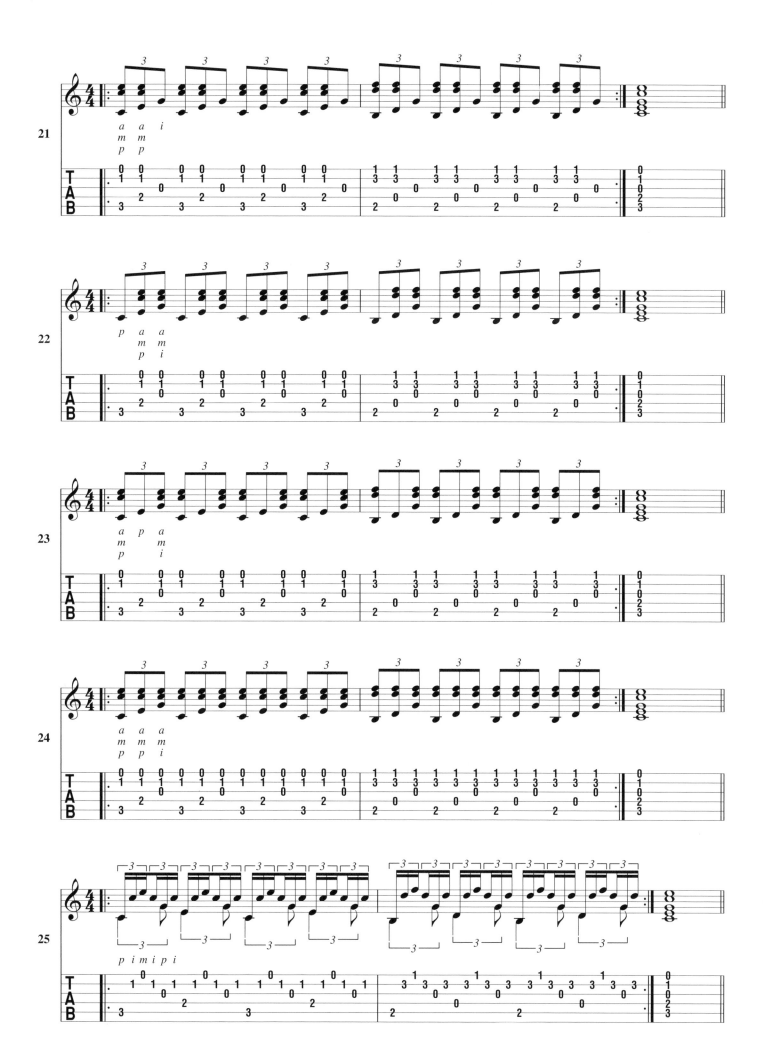

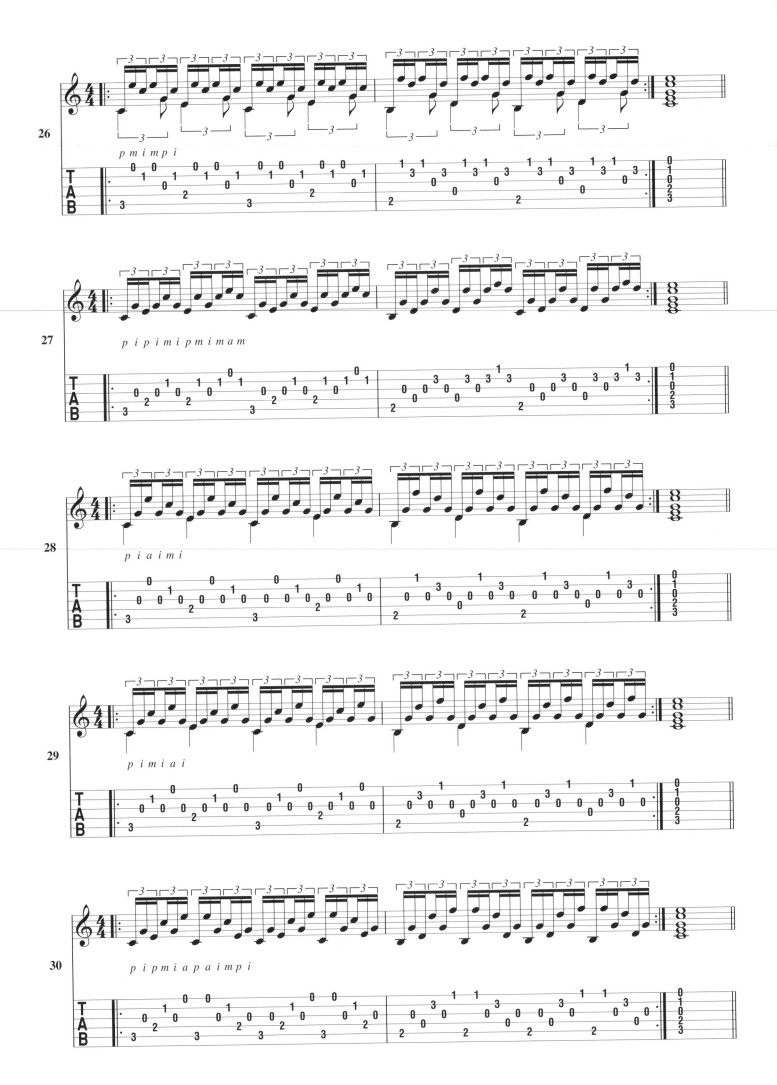

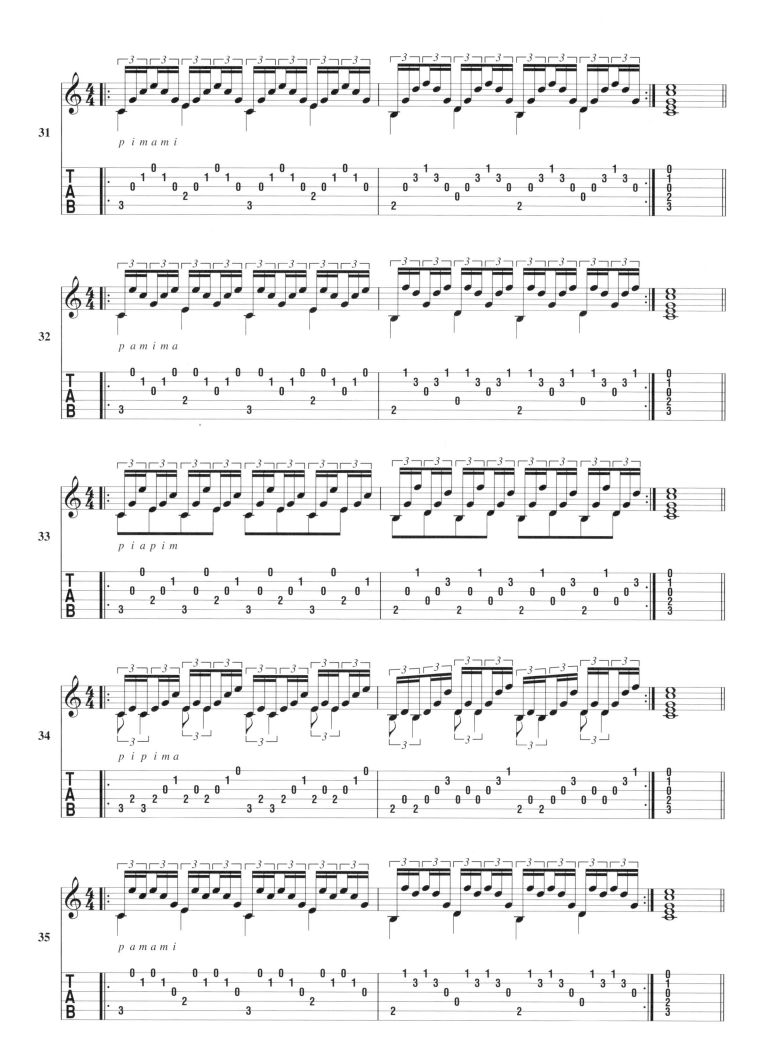

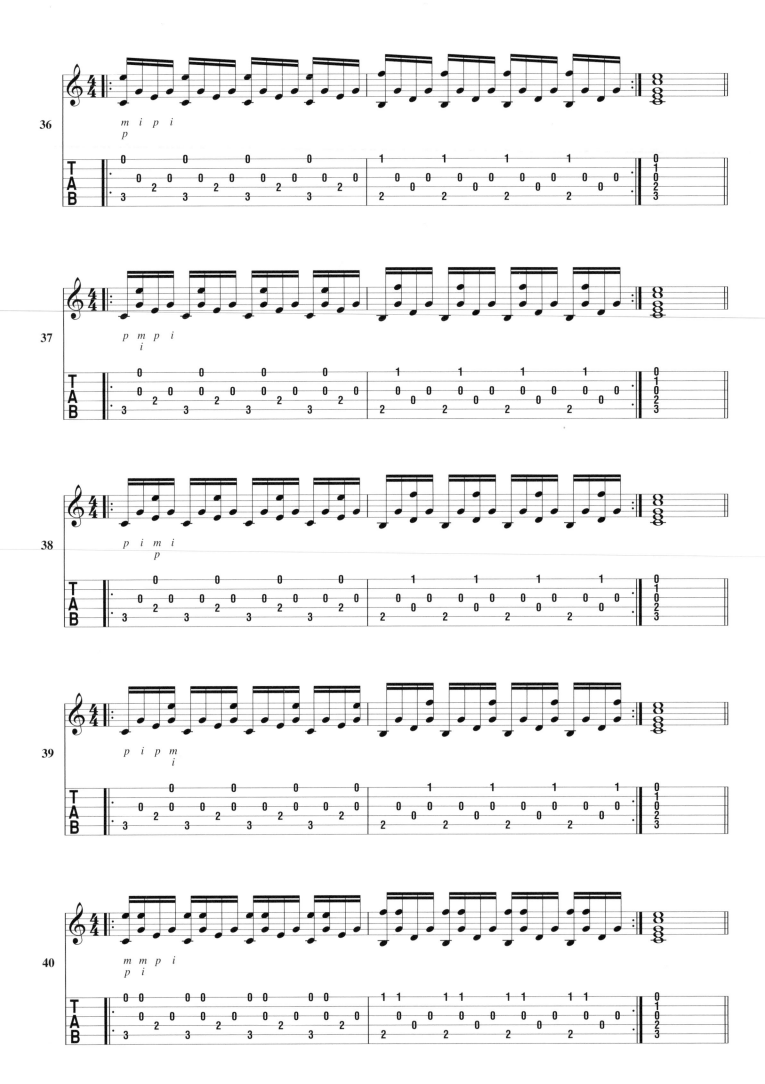

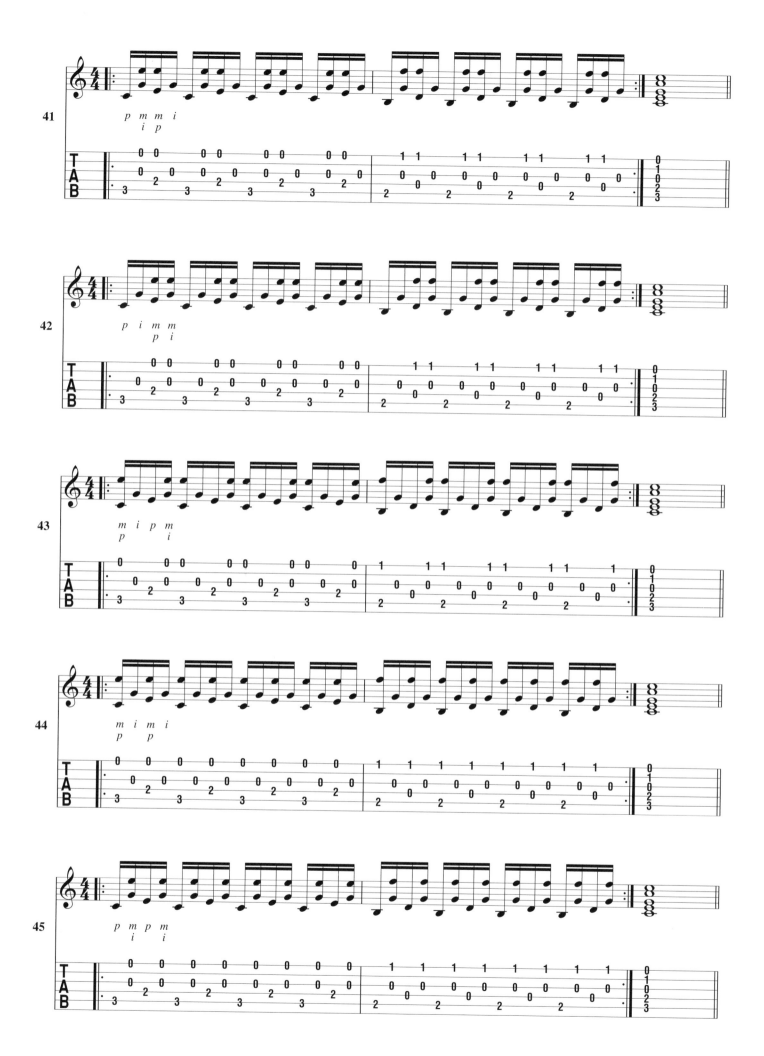

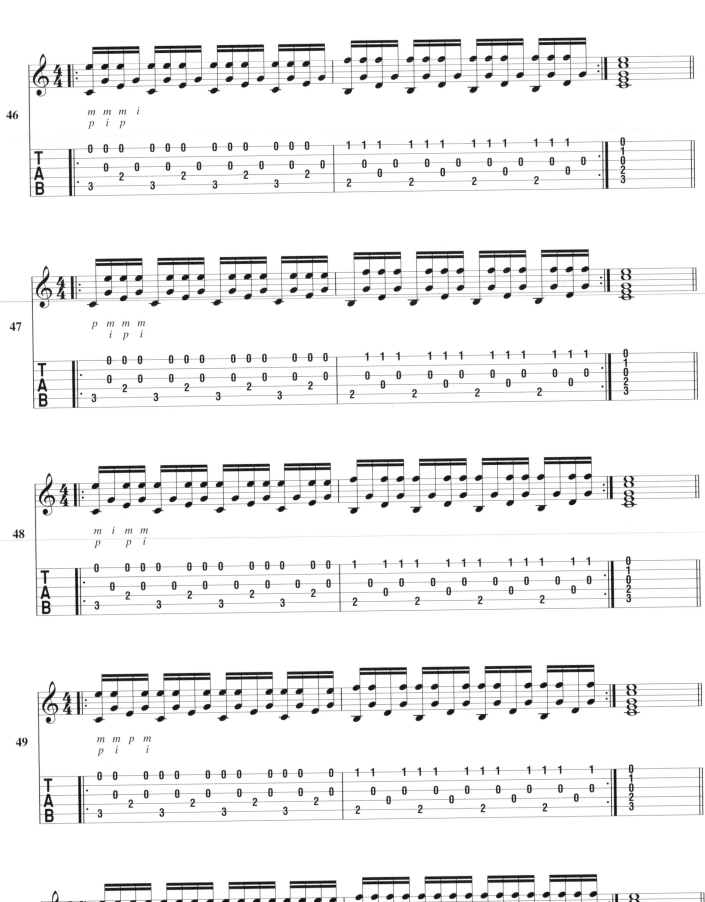

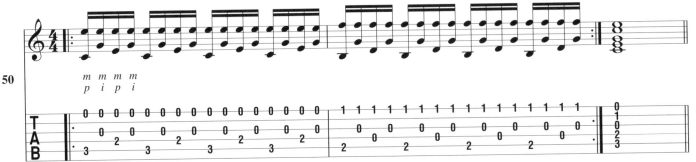

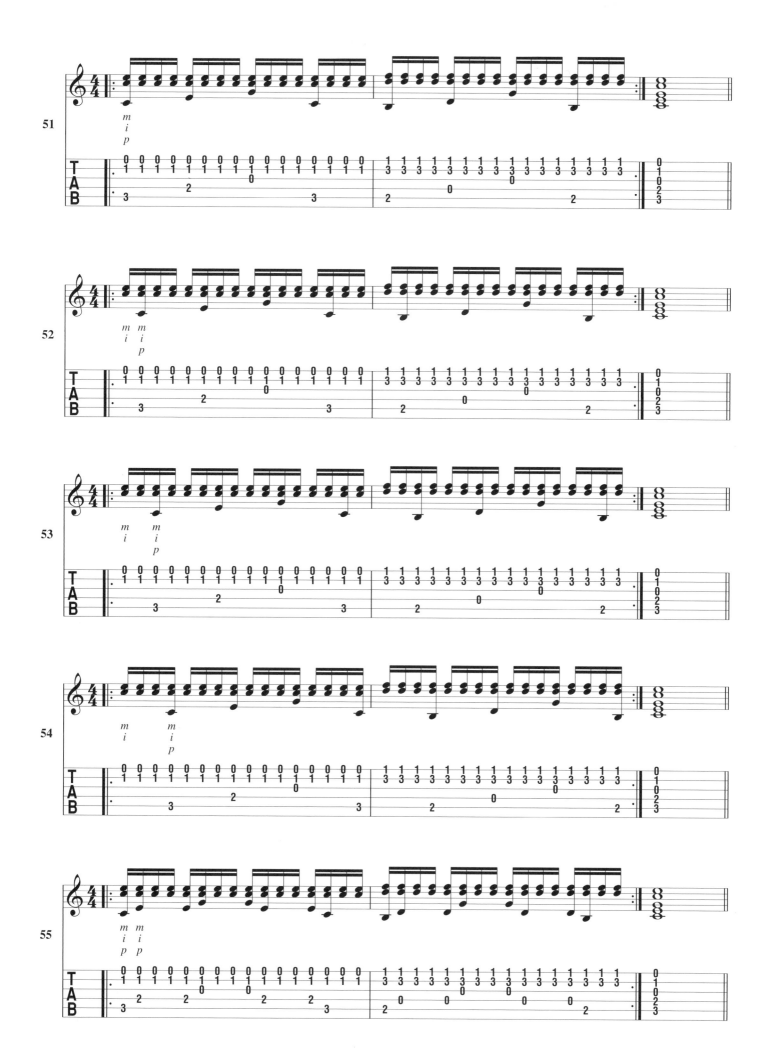

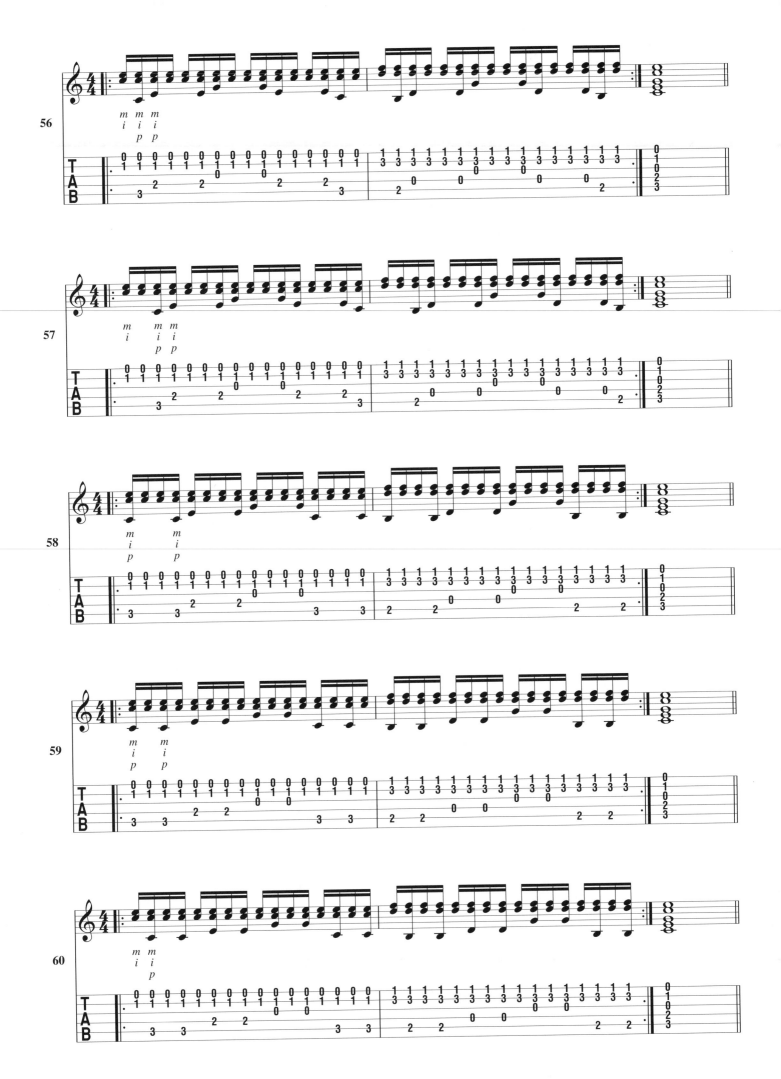

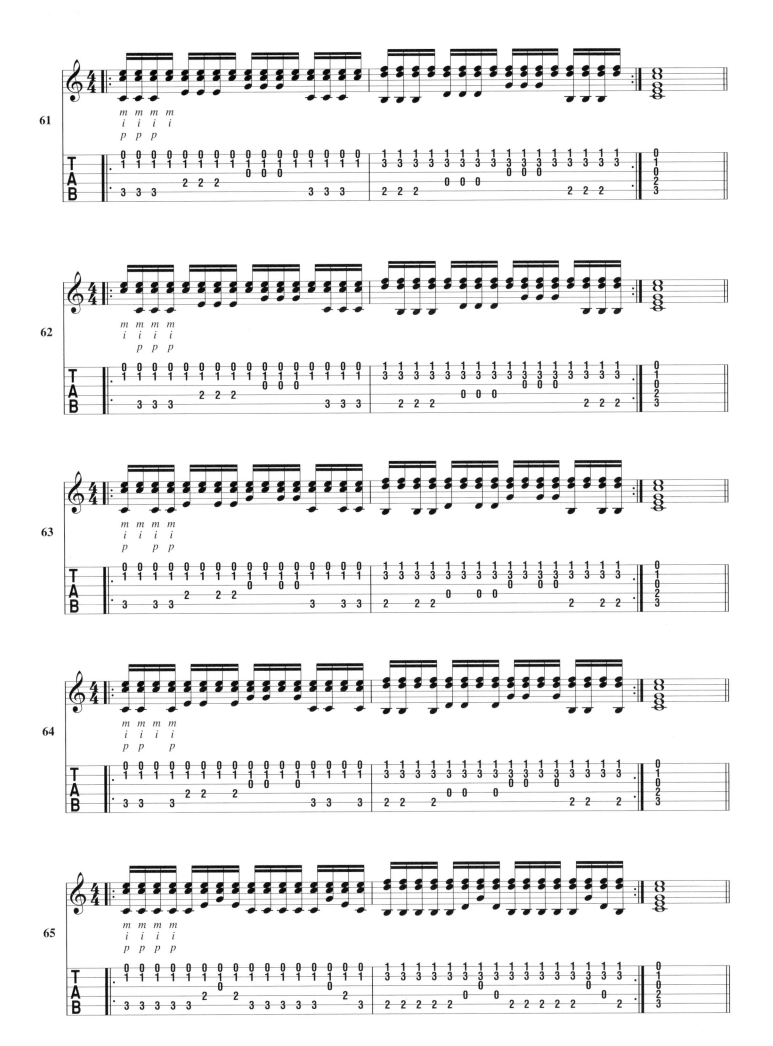

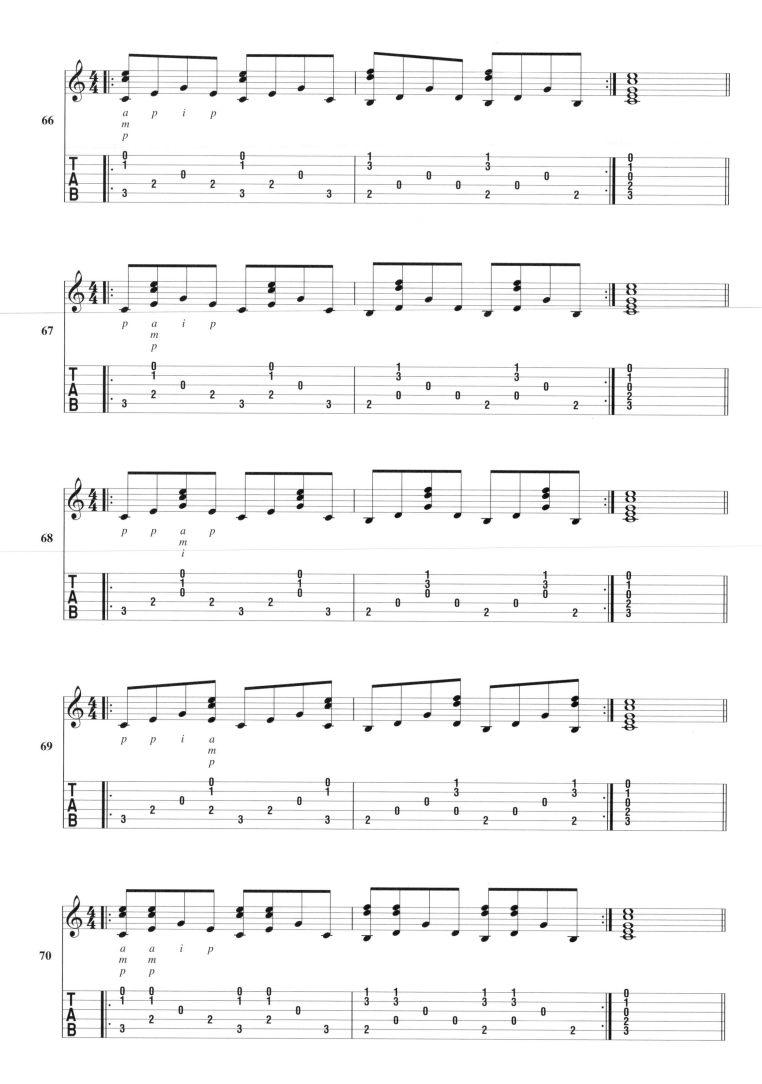

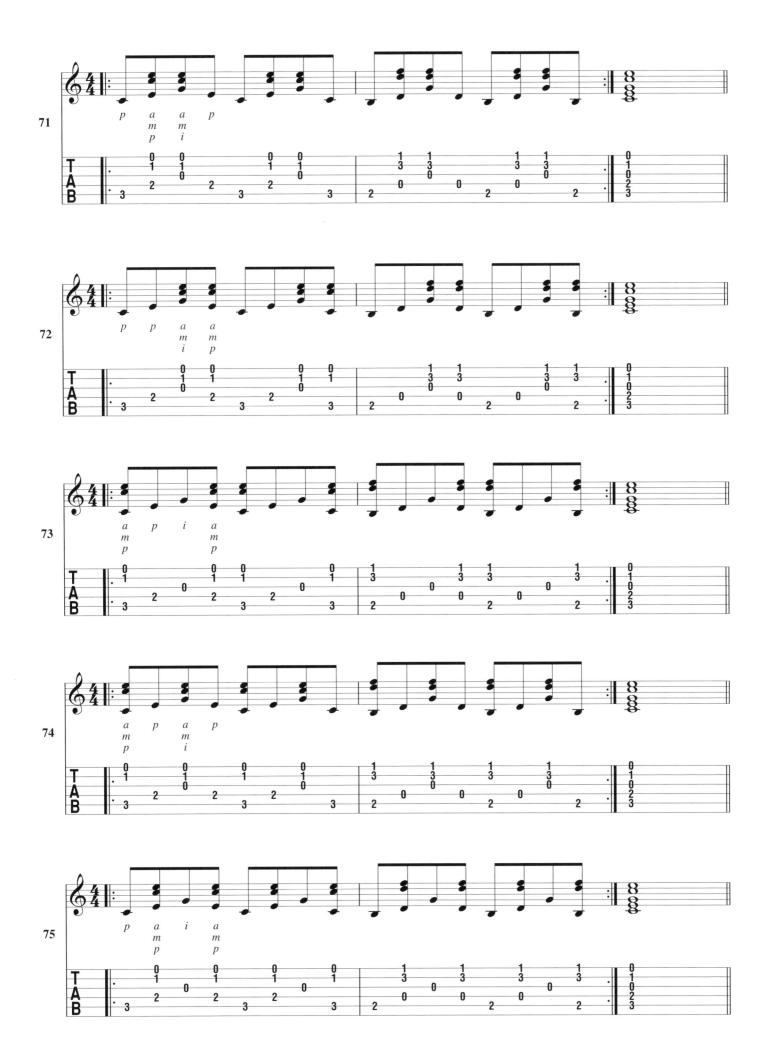

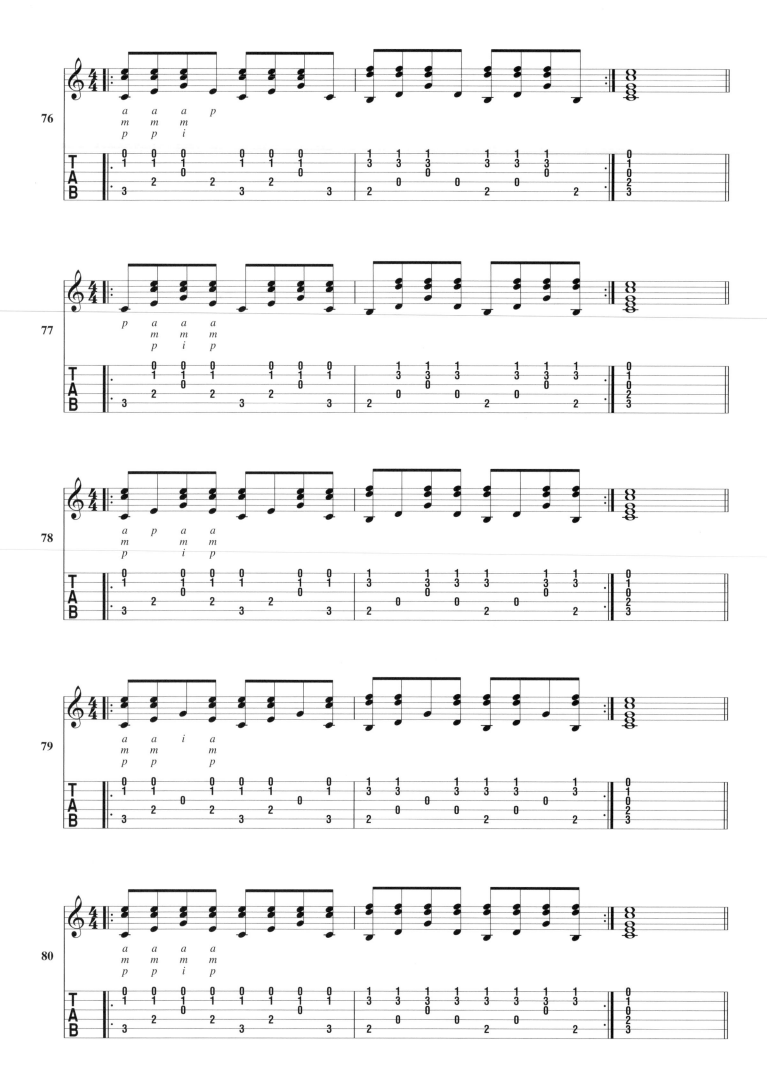

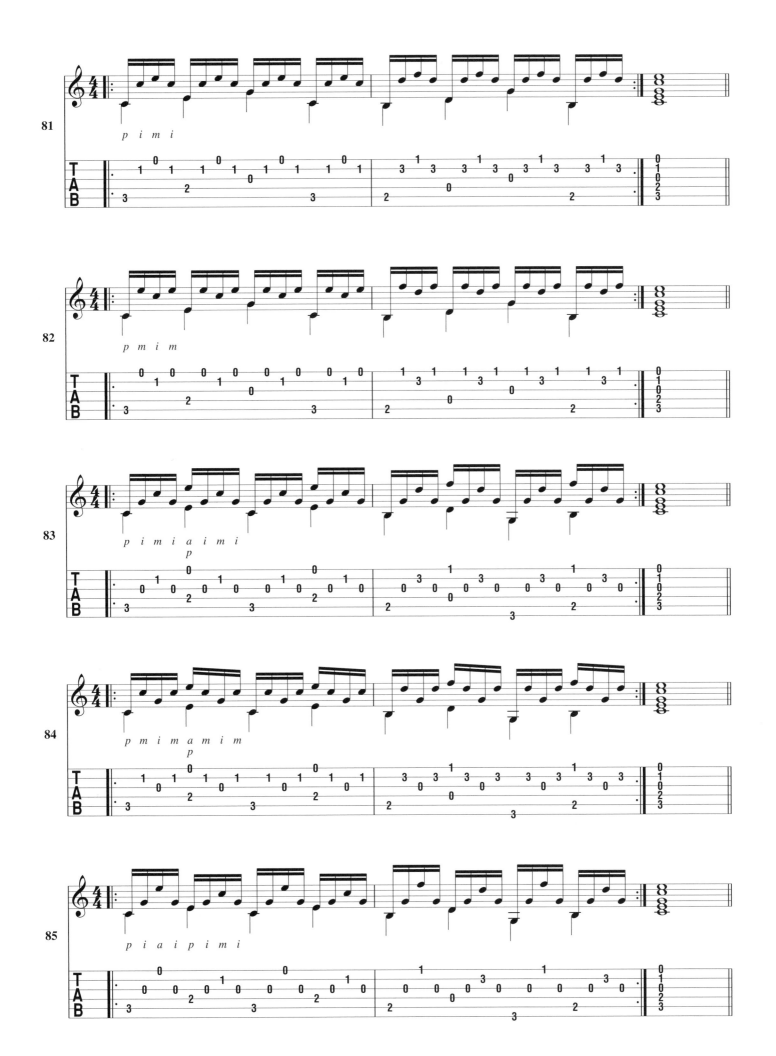

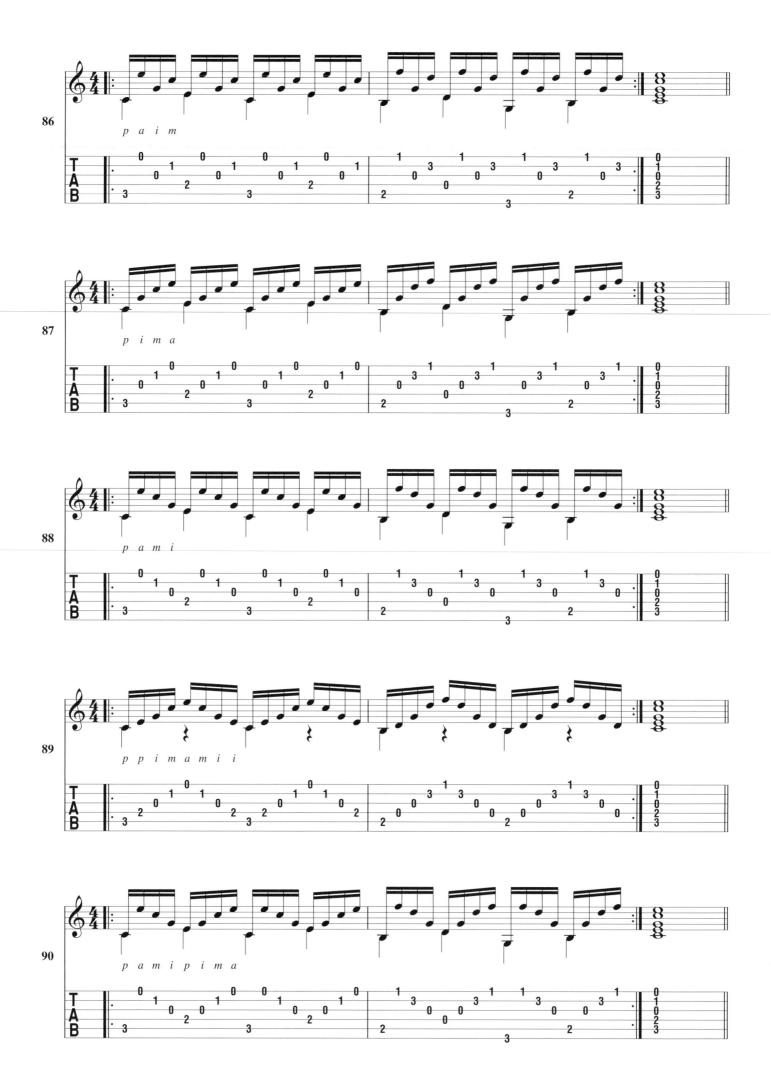

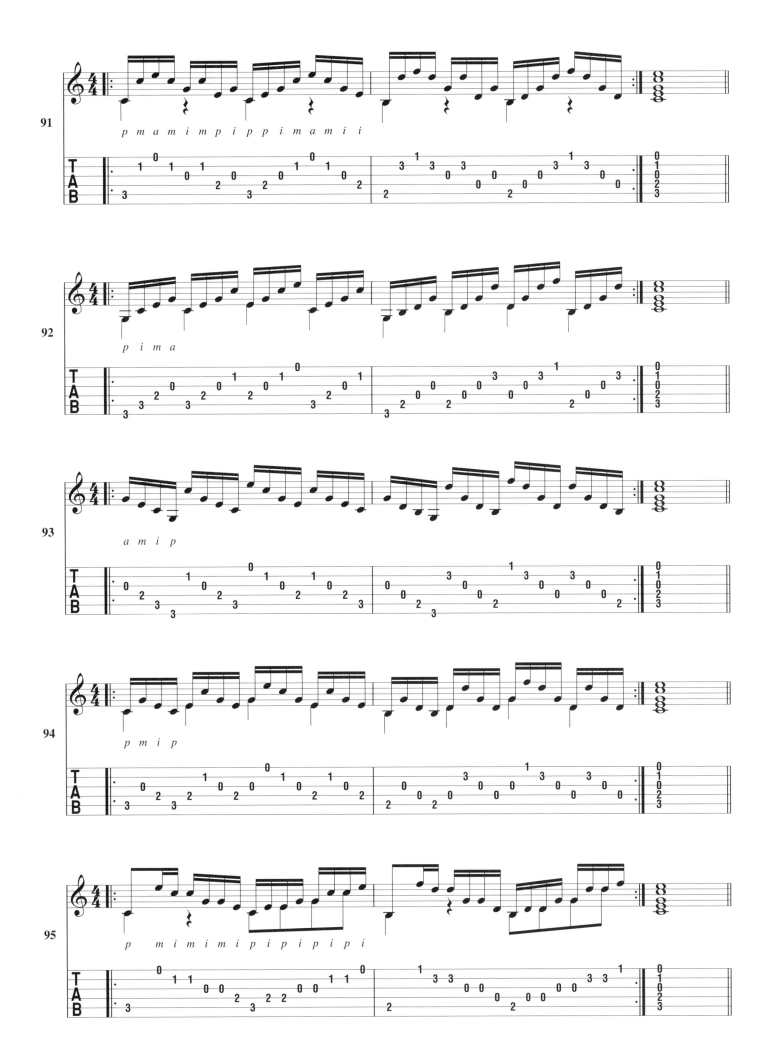

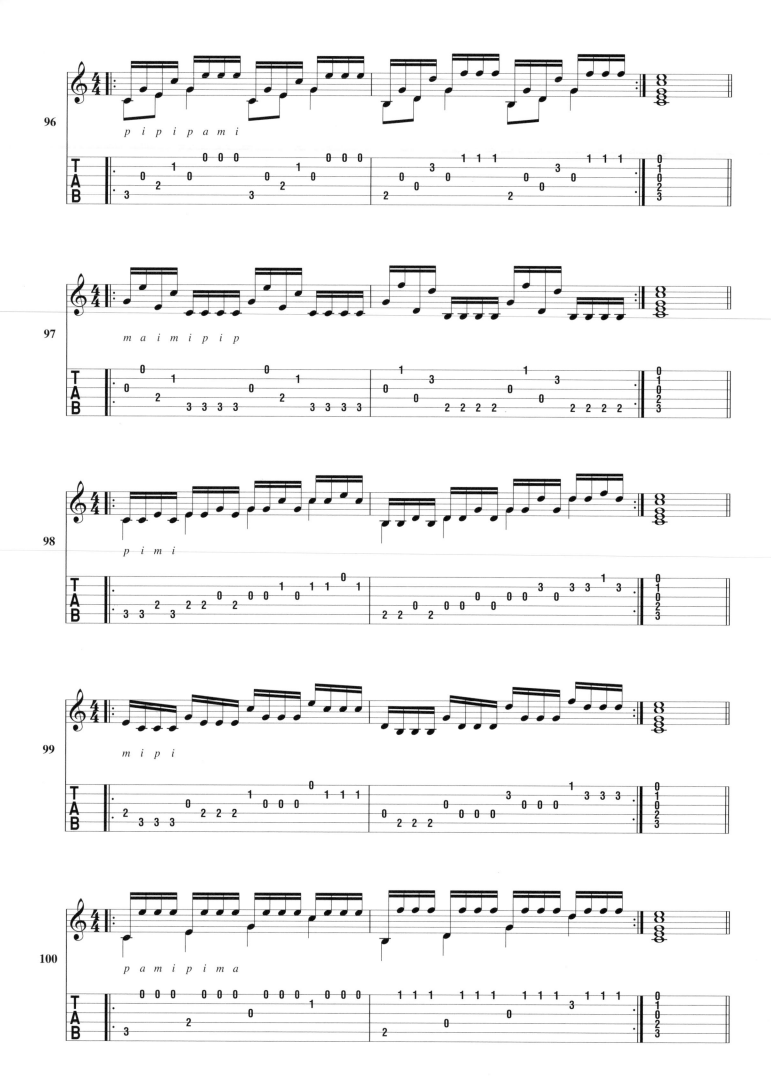

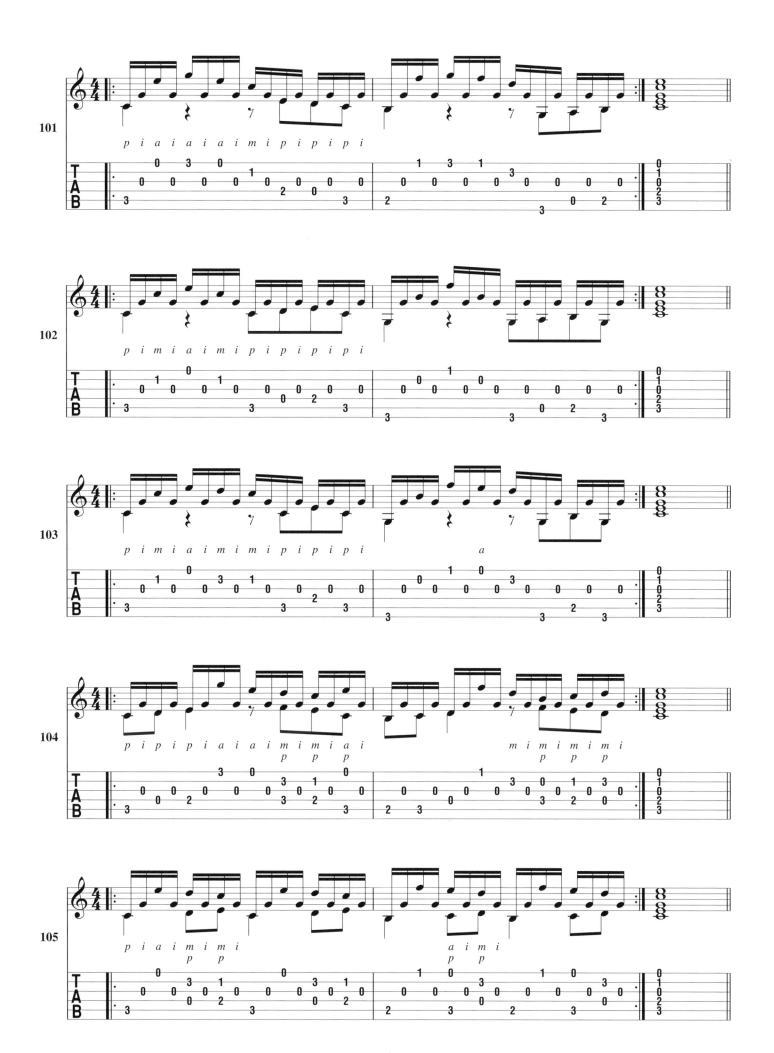

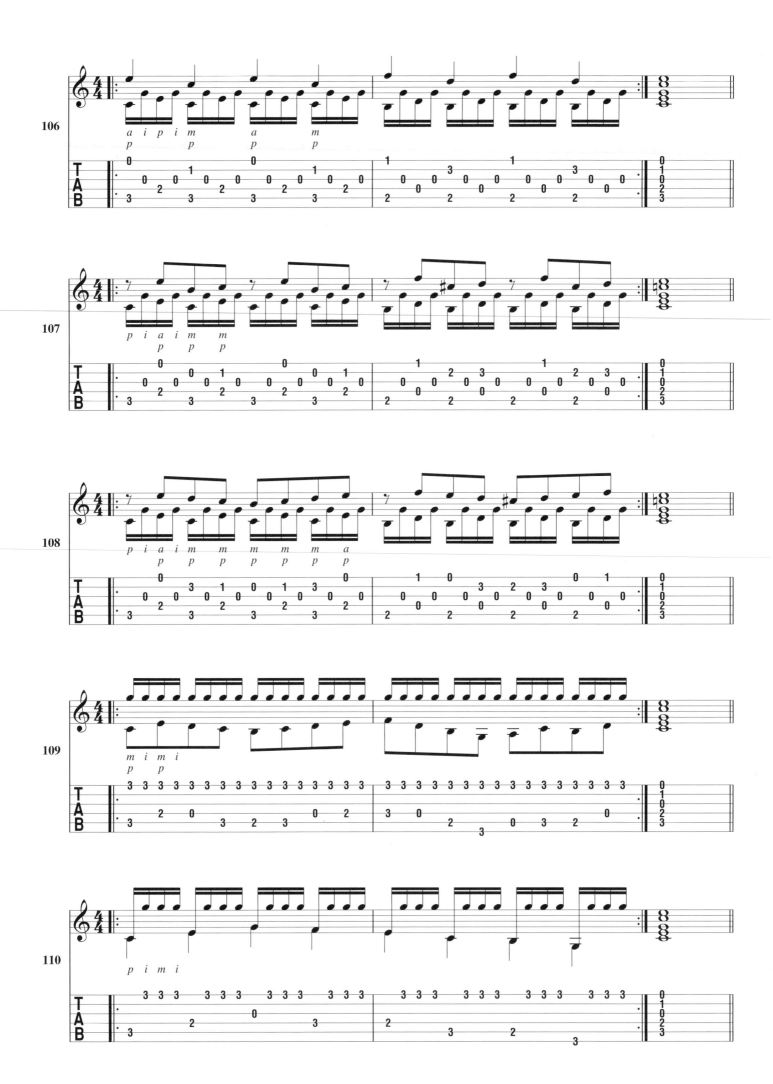

84

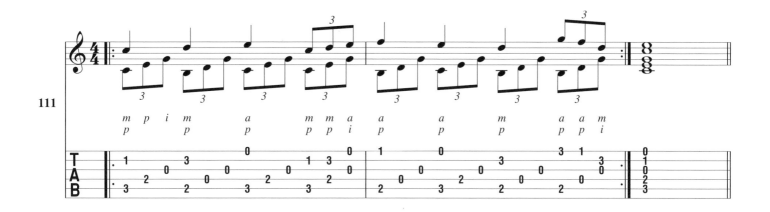

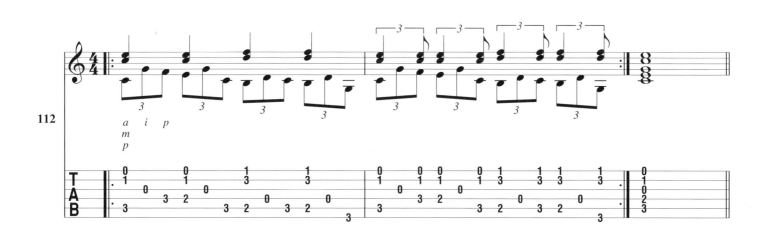

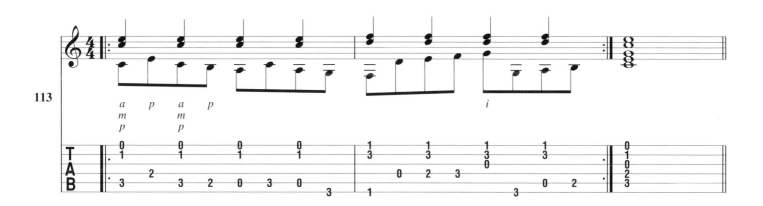

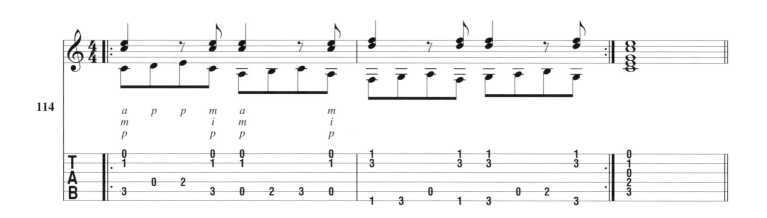

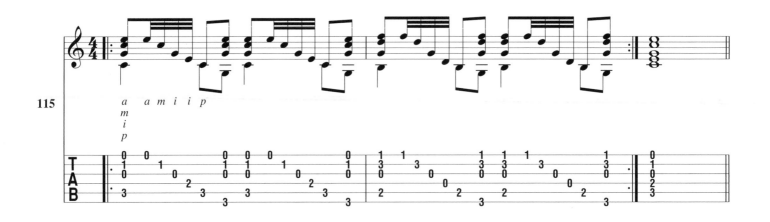

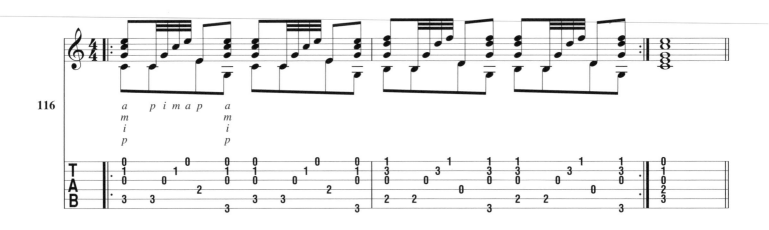

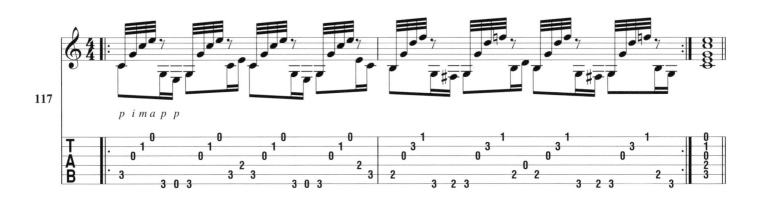

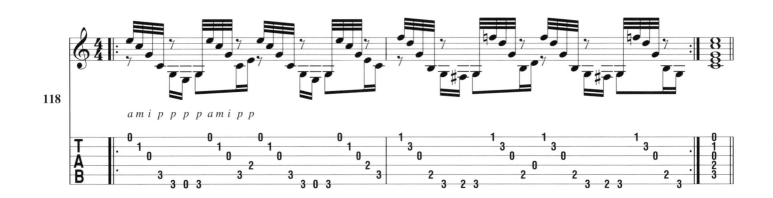

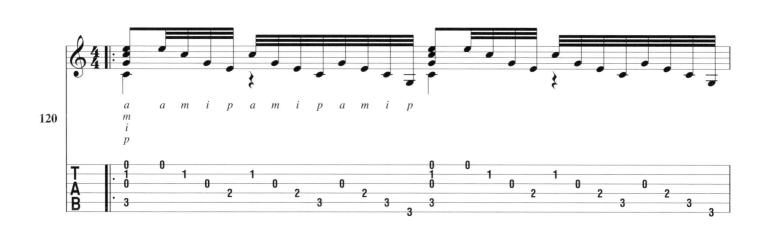

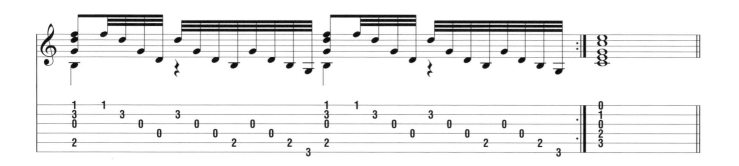

Ascending and Descending Slur Exercises

Francisco Tárrega

These slur exercises are a great way to warm up your left-hand fingers. Each example focuses solely on ascending slurs (hammer-ons) or descending slurs (pull-offs). Practice moving each pattern up the fingerboard chromatically. Alternate your right-hand *i* and *m* fingers. I highly recommend using varying left- and right-hand fingers for these patterns. For example, in the first exercise, you could use your left-hand 2nd and 3rd fingers or 3rd and 4th fingers to hammer each two-note grouping. Strive for evenness between the right- and left-hand articulations.

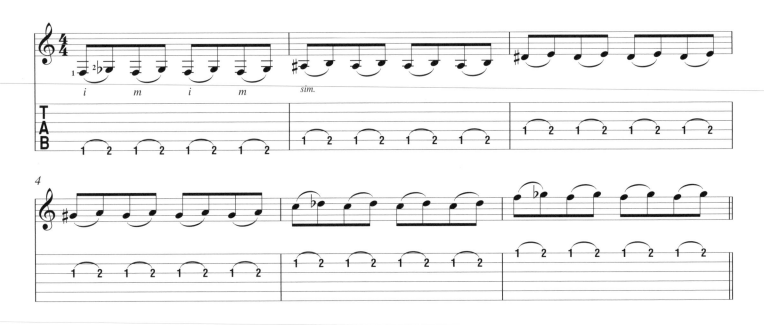

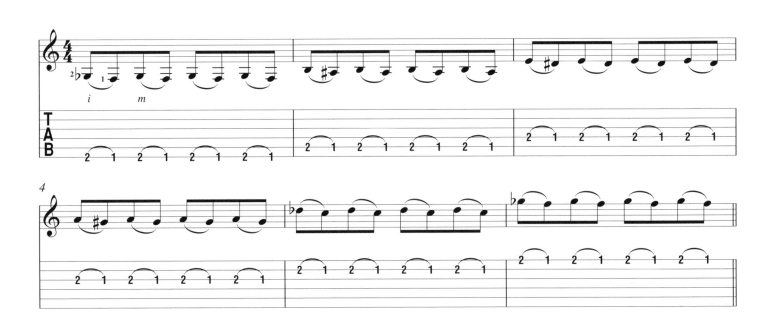

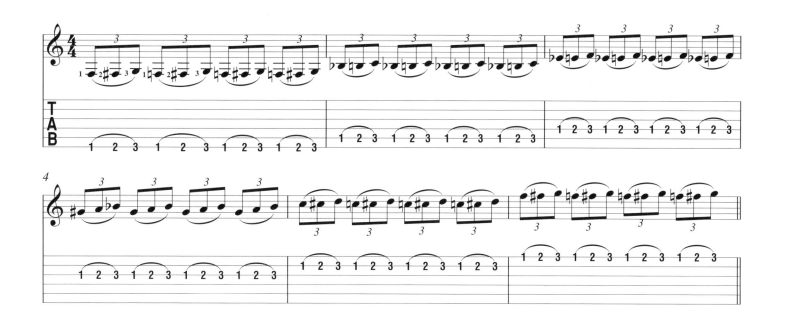

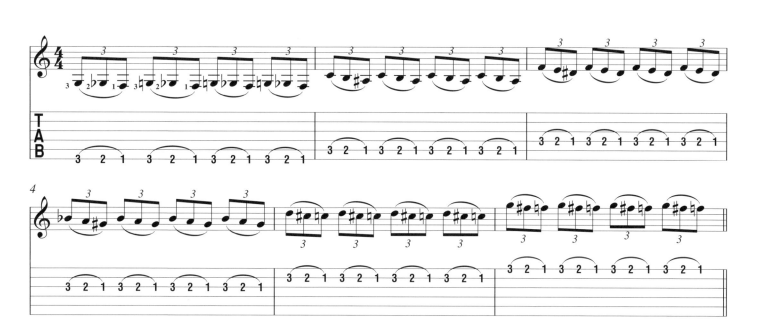

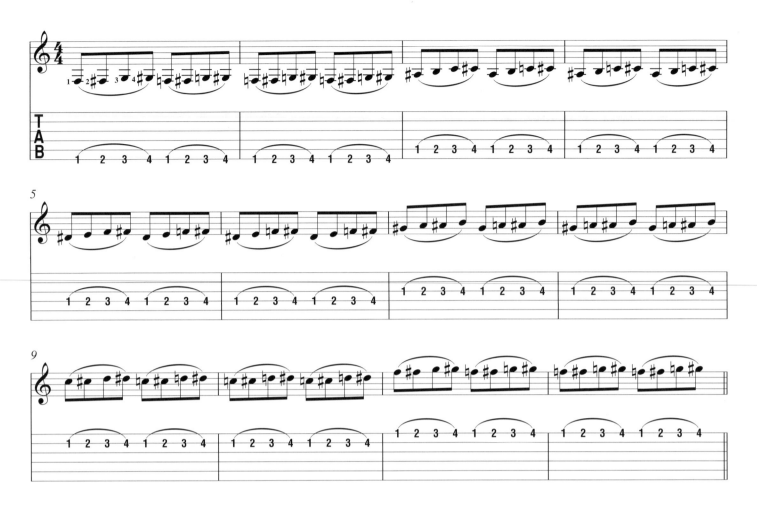

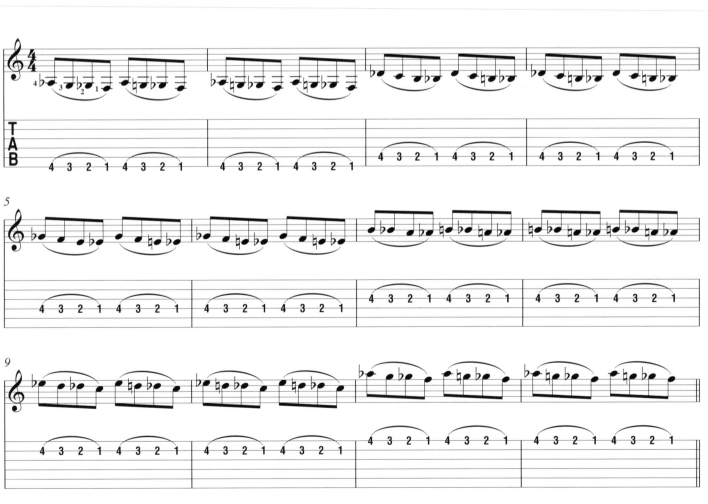

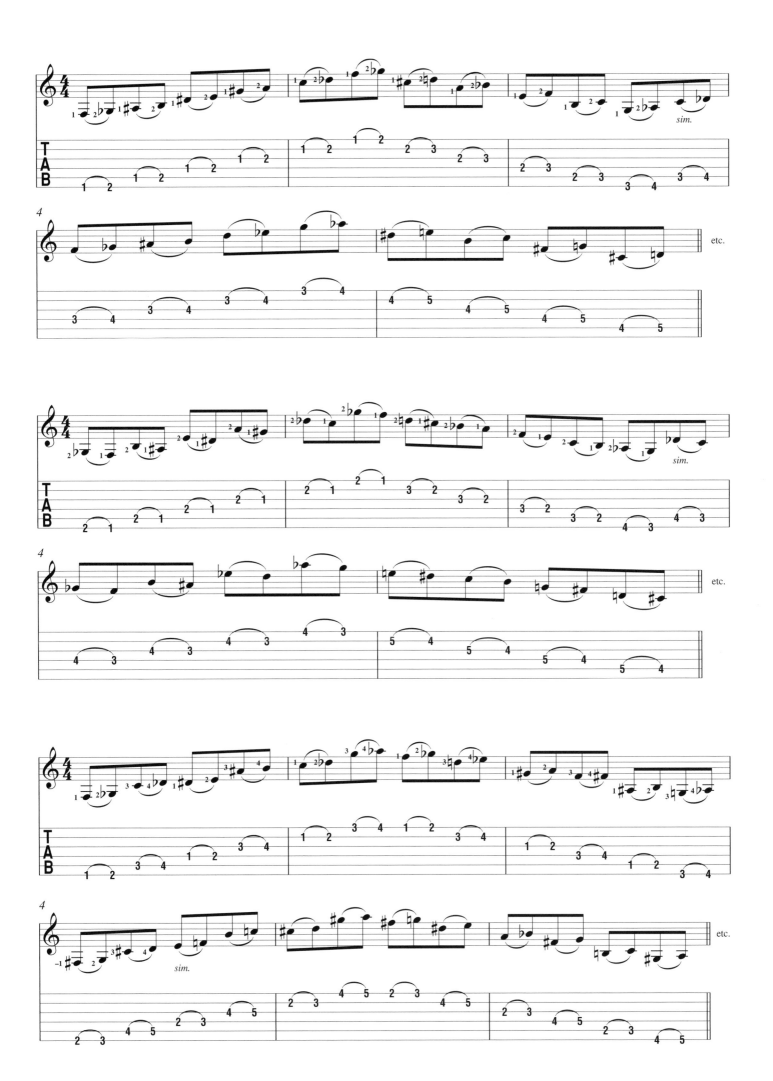

Intervallic Arpeggio Exercises

Mauro Giuliani

Giuliani's intervallic exercises in 3rds, 6ths, octaves, and 10ths require quick left-hand motions to produce connectivity between the notes, so prepare your fingers ahead of time whenever possible. Once you learn Giuliani's left-hand fingerings, experiment with your own. It's not always easy, but there is great value in practicing his fingering choices. If you look at the first example, you could easily change the first two notes to your 3rd and 2nd fingers, which would allow you to prepare your 1st finger for the following B note. Practice this exercise by repeating *p-i* for the right-hand pattern or by alternating between *p-i* and *p-m*.

3RDS

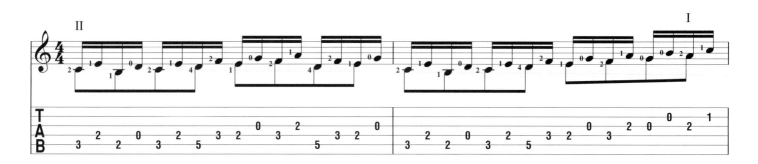

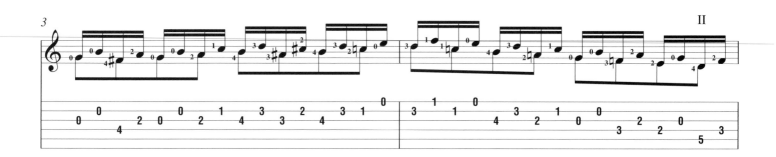

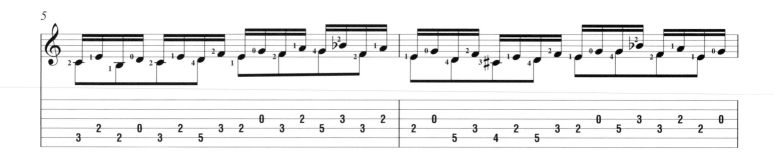

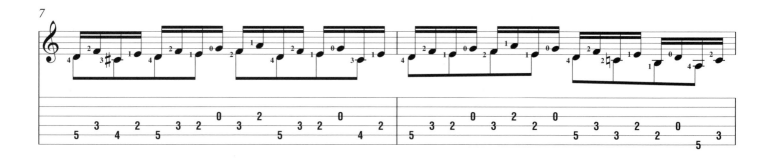

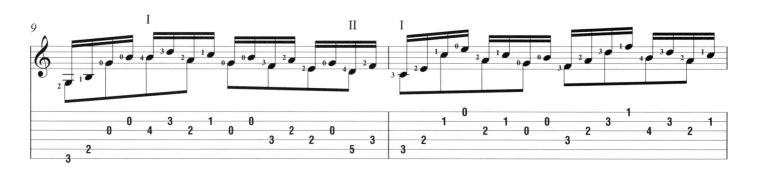

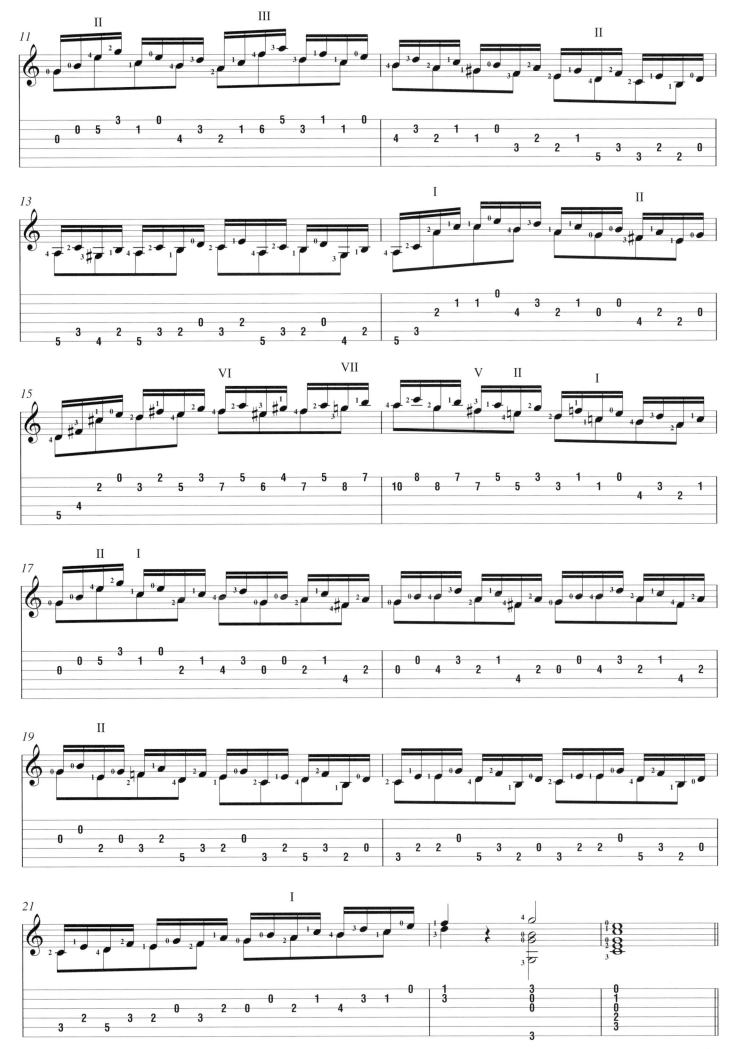

6THS

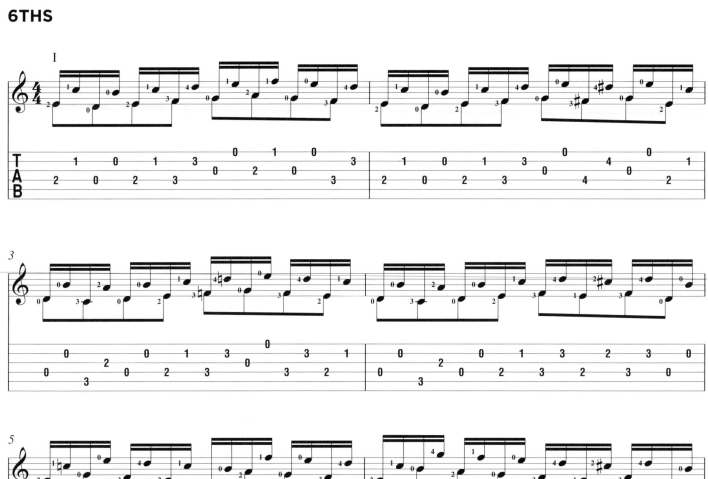

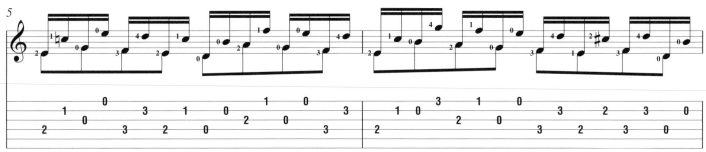

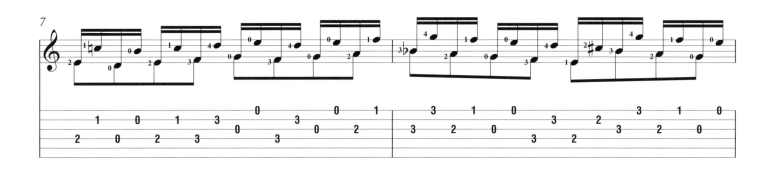

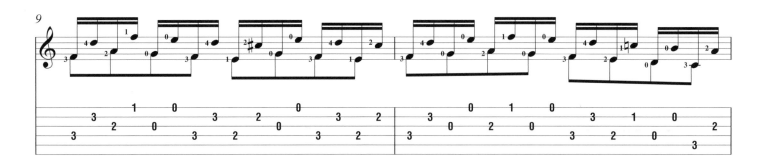

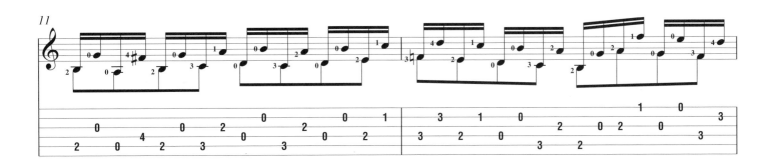

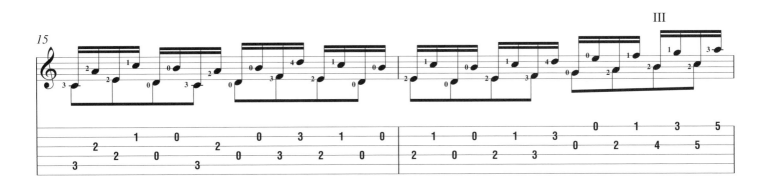

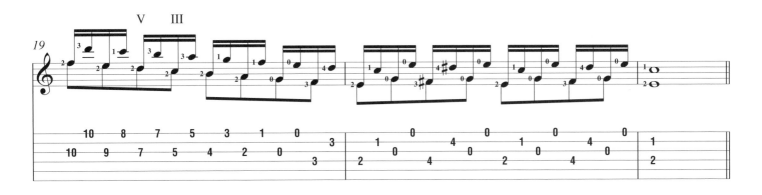

OCTAVES

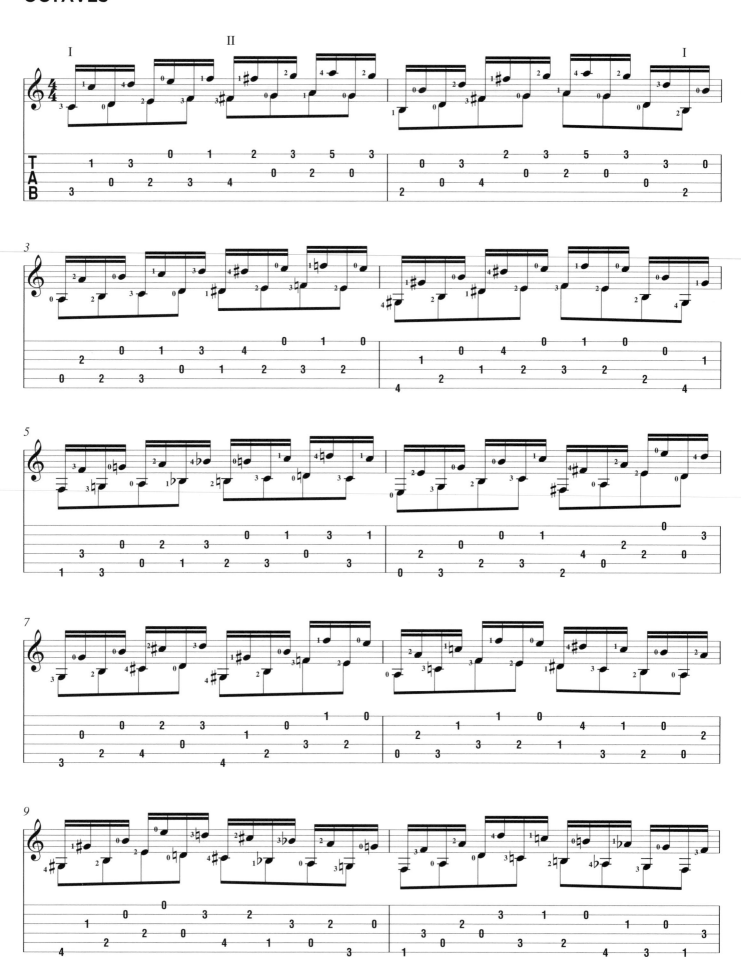

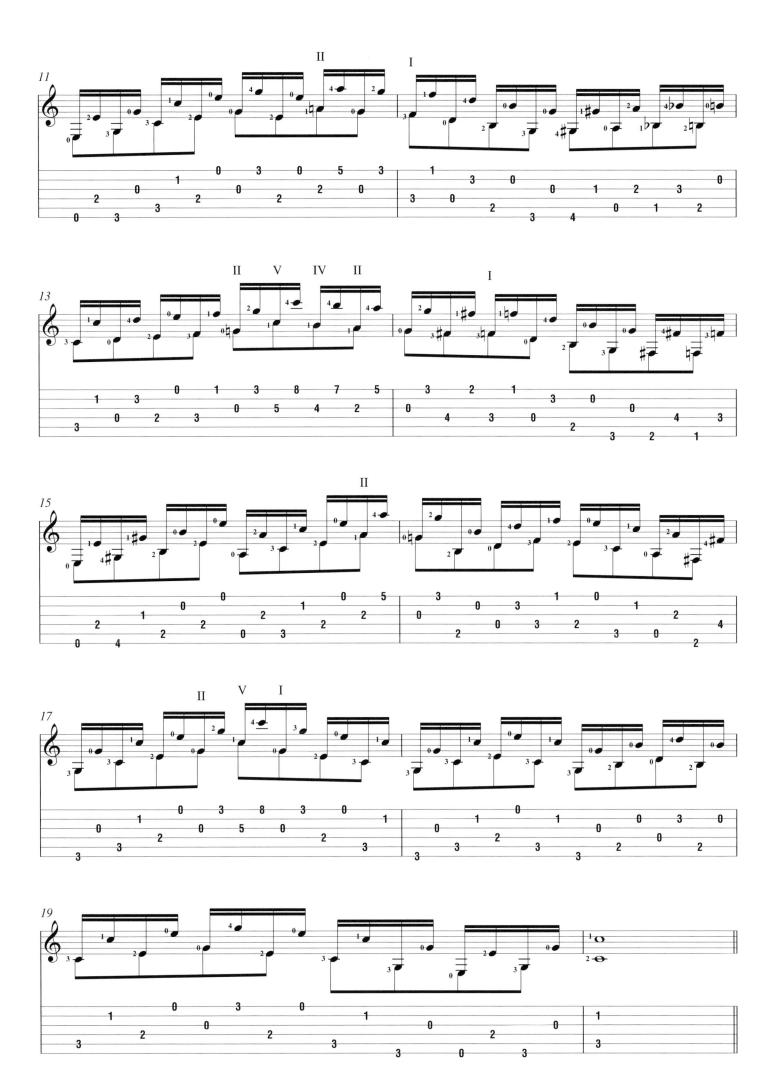

10THS

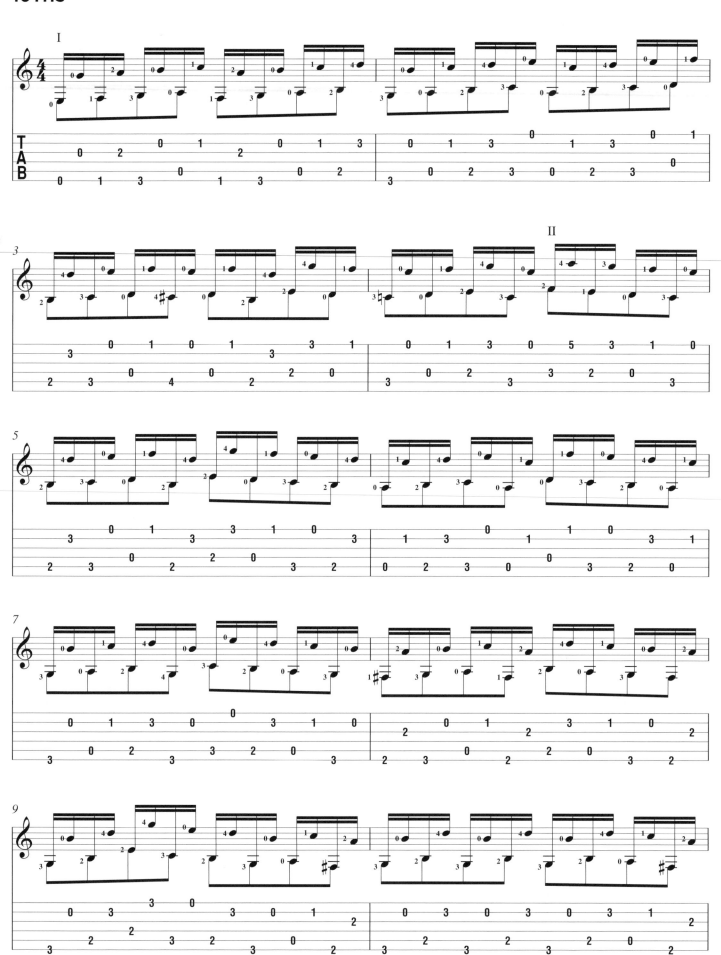

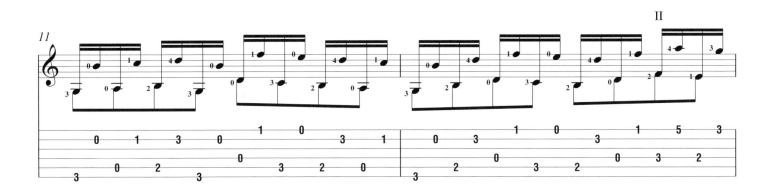

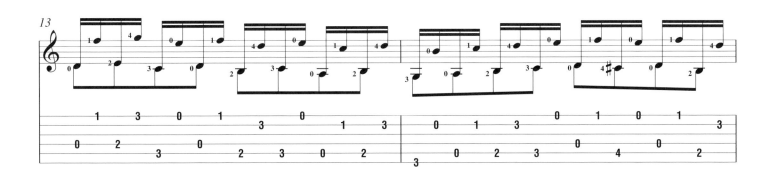

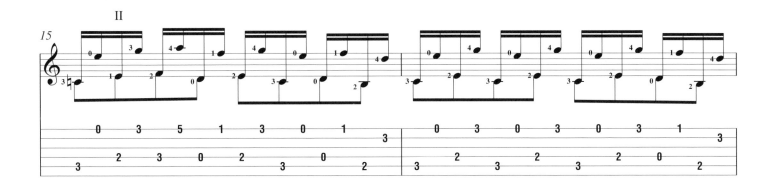

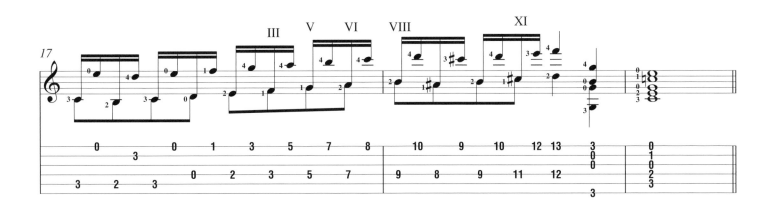

Scales in Intervals

Matteo Carcassi

These scales and exercises in 3rds, 6ths, octaves, and 10ths require some challenging left-hand motions. In the previous Giuliani intervallic exercises, there is more time to prepare your left-hand fingers ahead of each movement, since each note is separate. But the following examples require intervals (dyads) to be plucked simultaneously, thus limiting the time available between each subsequent shift. To connect the notes, it will be important to keep your motions small and quick. Release tension as much as possible in every movement. Different combinations of right-hand fingers can be used to execute these examples, such as *p* and *i* or *i* and *m*.

6THS

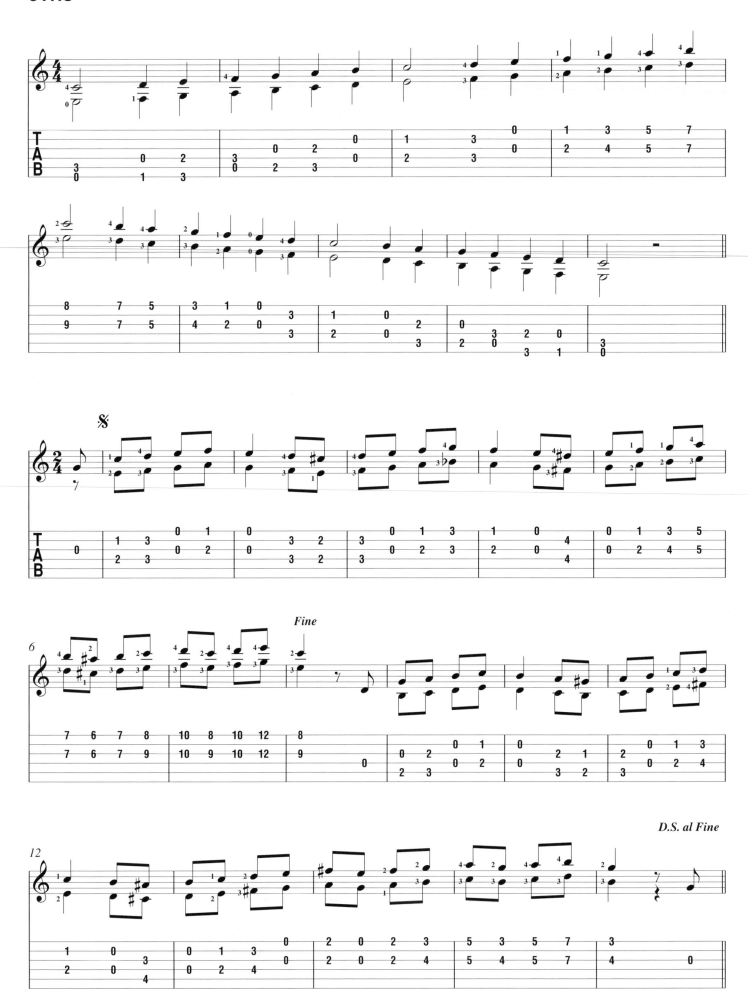

OCTAVES

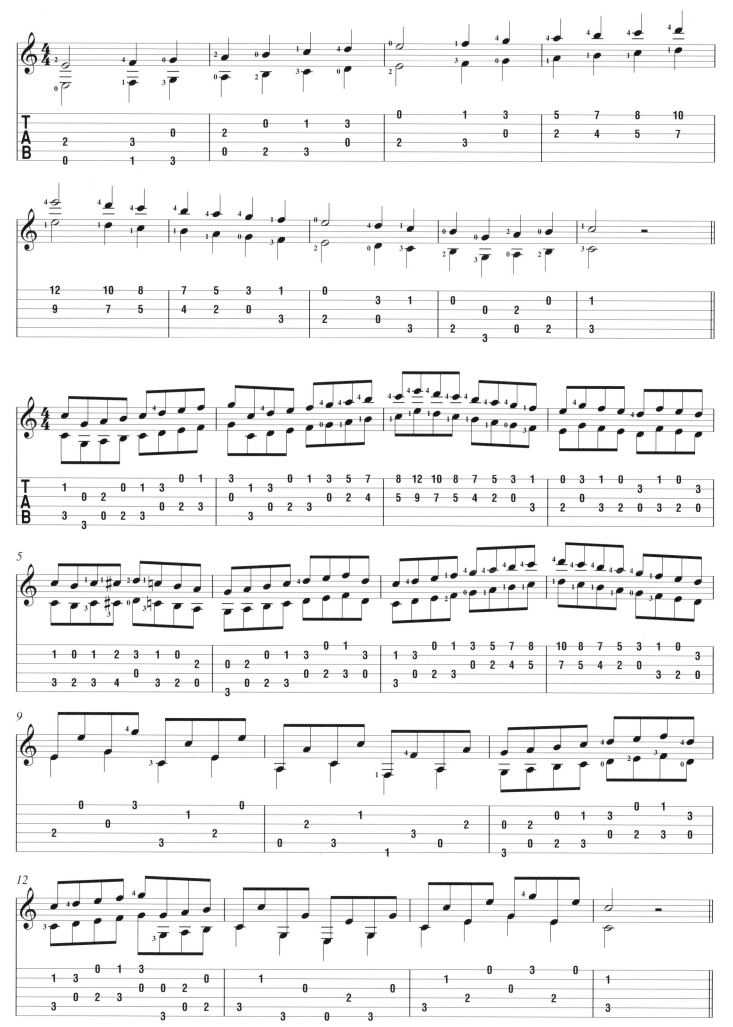

10THS

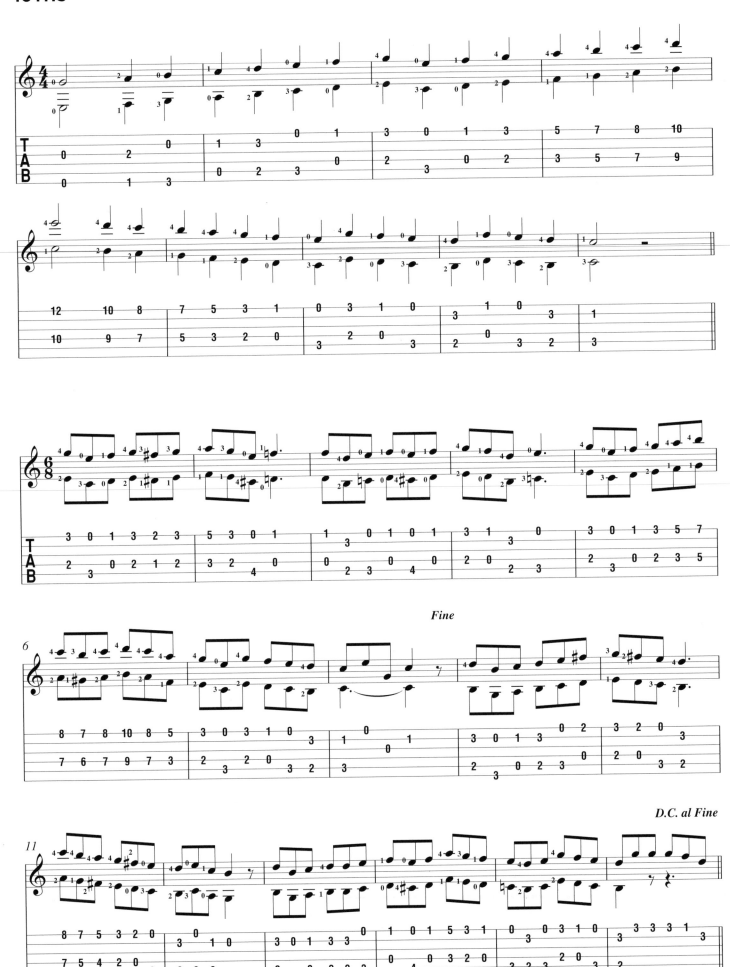